Date Due

The Business of Show Business

The Business
of
Show Business

GAIL PLUMMER

HARPER & BROTHERS, PUBLISHERS, NEW YORK

THE BUSINESS OF SHOW BUSINESS

FIRST EDITION

Library of Congress catalog card number: 61–7923

CONTENTS

FOREWORD

Paul Gregory
Gregory Enterprises, Inc.

This book will be a boon not only to theatre people but to every manager and promoter of entertainments of all kinds and sizes. It is a compendium of the most sensible and effective money saving and money getting ideas in show business. Here is a forthright, comprehensive presentation of problems and answers beginning with the conception of the first plans to the final audit.

I know the author well and have done business with him over a ten-year period. He does not try to outsmart either his customers or his associates. His ability to sell a show and keep it in the black is well known. His book is based on more than twenty-five years of experience.

PREFACE

Positively the weakest link in the chain of public entertainment is the promotion and management. That this statement is a cliché with a beard, only emphasizes the seriousness of a problem which exists everywhere among theatres, symphonies, operas, lectures, concerts, and movies. Nor is there much consolation in the paradox that we have an excellent supply of well trained actors, singers, directors, conductors, and designers.

By comparison there is a real shortage of talent and literature in show business per se. Artists and actors are primarily interested in their art which concerns the stage. To most of them the business side of the theatre is mere drudgery, something like peeling the potatoes or washing the dishes. It should be assigned to the artless, the dull and the untalented. Such a fallacy is a costly one. In communities of all sizes excellent talent has been available but because no one knew enough or cared enough about the vital organ of management, their theatres collapsed. Contrary to the common belief, the field of management is not dull but loaded with excitement and challenges which call for the use of imagination. Can one think of the life of P. T. Barnum as dull?

For more than twenty-five years I have been collecting thousands of ideas from professional and amateur show business people. This book is an attempt to sift and arrange those ideas under a system of labels that others may find useful.

Because I could find only limited information in the libraries and books, I gathered it from many other sources. As a manager of a large, university auditorium, I booked a variety of professional traveling shows which proved to be excellent sources of information on show business. Some were strong in one phase and some in others. Whatever trade secrets these troupes may have had they never withheld them. There was stimulating material from Earl Carroll's Vanities, Stratford-on-Avon Company, Fortune Gallo's, San Carlo operas, Ballet Russe and other ballets, Walter Hampden, Katherine Cornell and Paul Gregory and Associates, and many others.

Because much of the information from the professional field did not pertain to the amateur theatre, I began a series of inquiries by correspondence as to how university and community theatres handled their promotion and management. This correspondence was not too revealing and I utilized a year's leave and traveled over 5,000 miles during which time I visited over a hundred university and community theatres in various parts of the United States and Canada. This study was highly rewarding: I collected all kinds of questions and answers. Everywhere I was received most cordially. My University of Utah President, A. Ray Olpin, was kind enough to send letters to other universities which facilitated my getting complete information. The one thing that seemed to be borne out almost everywhere was that the quality of the productions was superior to the quality of the management. In only a few places could the promotion and management be called satisfactory. Practically all expressed a desire to improve this department of the theatre. Every theatre had at least one or two good ideas to pass along.

It had been my hope to find an easy way to manage and promote entertainment so that I could tell my friends about it. But all the ways I found were hard ways and none of the gimmicks were in any way automatic. Back of every successful operation I found many people working hard and putting in long hours. I am sorry to report that I found no easy way—not one.

It would be like reproducing the directory of the American Educational Theatre Association to list all who gave me ideas, encouragement, and suggestions. In my classes of theatre management were hundreds of students whose enthusiasm, optimism and originality were stimulating and contagious. Such young people can be invaluable to any theatre. Not to train and use them is to lose one of the greatest human resources. Even at the risk of leaving out important contributors, I must express thanks to the following: H. D. Albright, Campton Bell, Francis Cary Bowen, Robert R. Case, Edward Cole, Richard Dunham, Nat Eek, Joseph C. Fitch, Theodore Fuchs, Robert Gard, Harold I. Hansen, Rev. G. V. Hartke, Hubert Heffner, Glen Hughes, Paul Kozelka, Peter R.

Marroney, Albert Mitchell, Jack Morrison, T. Earl Pardoe, John Parker, Norman Philbrick, James E. Popovich, Horace W. Robinson, Aaron Roylance, Samuel Selden, Claude L. Shaver, Milton Smith, John Wesley Swanson, Twain Tippitts, Hal J. Todd, Lillian W. Vorhees, Fairfax Proudfit Walkup, Frank M. Whiting, and John Wray Young.

The American Educational Theatre Association, American National Theatre and Academy, Northwest Theatre Conference, and the Rocky Mountain Theatre Conference have given extensive aid and encouragement to the project. Appreciation is extended to the members of the University of Utah Theatre staff, especially to Dr. Ralph Margetts who designed the article, "A Prop for the Fainting Budget." Dr. George Osborne, formerly with the University of Utah School of Pharmacy, and now at the University of Rhode Island, prepared the article, "The Small Scale Manufacture of Theatrical Cosmetics." Two men who worked closely with me, Royal C. Miller as box office manager, and Joseph Naffzinger as auditor were counselors on tickets and budgets. Mr. and Mrs. Larry Shumate have given valuable assistance in the art work.

Without the assistance of my son, Tom; my daughter, Bonnie; and my wife, Elva, the work could not have been completed.

Last and by no means least I extend grateful acknowledgments for the patience and skill of Lousene Rousseau and Ordway Tead of Harper & Brothers.

PART ONE

Before the Show

SELECTING A PLAY OR A SEASON OF PLAYS

Choosing a play is in many respects like choosing a wife. If you choose wisely, the road ahead will be smooth; the hours will not drag; your theatre may even be financially successful.

But now hear this: If you choose the wrong play (or wife) for any appeasement, intimidation, snap judgment, in-law interference, plain ignorance, desperation, or wounded vanity, then surely you have successfully courted failure—and one of three bad alternatives remains:

1. If the choice is not wholly wrong but only partially so and love grows, the troubles may possibly be resolved.

2. But if the problems are great and the love is thin, and still you stick philosophically to your choice, the way will be hard, the end bitter.

3. Should you decide that you cannot possibly go on with your choice of the play, that you must drop it completely and choose another, then embarrassment and expense will follow as surely as the sun sets.

Will your next choice be any better? Can you afford to continue the trial-and-error method? Anyway you look at it, a bad choice makes a bad start for which nothing can fully compensate.

Many people would like to believe that selection of the right play is nothing more than a piece of pure luck, and that you never can tell what will succeed and what will fail. They regard theatrical success to be as purely accidental as a game of roulette. Although it is true that no authority claims to possess a magic formula for play selection, the choice need not be left entirely to chance, to the "hazard of a die."

Successful producers, publishers, authors, directors, and managers will be the first to admit that they do not know everything about play selection. The most astute publishers know that a sizable percentage of their plays has almost no appeal and even though the element of chance runs high, they would not concede that little is known about the problem. They make it their business to find out all they can so that they can stay in business. Theatre producers must reduce the element of chance.

A little honest study and a willingness to look at the question without prejudice will help a great deal. Just because one cannot eliminate all the elements of chance, should not keep him from eliminating the obvious ones.

From the much that has been said by experts on the difficult question of "What play shall I produce?" the following data gleaned from experience may serve as a guide to play selection:

1. *Consider the audience.* Oscar Wilde, after viewing a first night failure of one of his plays, facetiously said, "The play was a success, but the audience was a failure." That this remark was merely a wisecrack has been proved by his successful plays wherein he considered the audience with great care. You cannot possibly know too much about your patrons. Although audiences have much in common, they also have sharp differences. Some simply will not tolerate such stage business as drinking or smoking. You may not like the public's reaction, but if you have this problem, you had better adjust to it realistically. A Broadway audience may not accept a play that has been successful in London. *The Vigil,* for instance, played two years in London but failed on Broadway. A similar fate befell *The Love of Four Colonels.* Broadway hits have sometimes failed in other American cities.

Every community, school, and church sets its own standards, tastes, prejudices, and dislikes. How does one find out what a given audience is prepared to appreciate and enjoy? The answer lies in ingenuity and observation. Study the people. Become acquainted with their background through the study of their newspapers, radio, churches, schools, and leaders. If they read, what is it? Get in tune with your prospective audience. Radio and television regard it necessary to spend millions of dollars to find what the listeners like. If your living theatre cannot afford to spend a little, it will not live. Ignorance of what your public wants is fatal. The Strategic Air Command posted a slogan which the theatre might adopt concerning its future. "What you don't know won't hurt you, it will kill you."

2. *Consider the available talent.* Some directors have been known to set their hearts on a play they cannot cast. If there is no one to play the title roles in *Hamlet, St. Joan, Hobson's Choice,* or *I Remember Mama,* the answer is to find something that comes within the realm of possibility. It may be an ambition to attempt to stage *The Medea* after seeing Judith Anderson interpret it. The idea presents a challenge similar to a hornet's nest. We may wish to imitate something which seems simple but which in reality is highly complicated.

3. *Get acquainted with many plays.* Examine with care those which may suit your particular theatre. Study the play publishers' catalogues. Visit the libraries which have drama collections. Check the *Burns Mantle Best Plays.* The last pages of these informative annuals include lists of plays and information about them which would be valuable for theatre directors in universities, colleges, high schools, and communities.

4. *Get a competent and willing playreading committee.* Let them make suggestions for your theatre. Unless such a steering committee is chosen with care—great care—it may steer you into trouble. Some people have little use for committees. One disillusioned man thus defined a committee: "A group of the unfit, appointed by the unwilling to do the unnecessary." Librarians and newspaper drama critics may be extremely helpful. Moreover, they are persuasive leaders to have on your team. The very existence of a well chosen reading committee will add prestige and improve publicity and public relations.

5. *Put some "name" plays on your season.* For example, in the theatre for young people, choose such titles as *The Wizard of Oz, Ali Baba and the Forty Thieves,* and *Cinderella.* Records show that they sell. We love the familiar melody, the familiar poem, and the familiar story. Sara Spencer, of The Children's Theatre Press, says, "Our experience is that boy titles have much more general appeal than girl titles, as girls are more willing to worship male heroes than boys are to accept the female of the species. For this reason, such titles as *Aladdin, Marco Polo, Daniel Boone, Hiawatha, Robinson Crusoe, Robin Hood, Oliver Twist, Hans Brinker, Huckleberry Finn, The Pied Piper, Rip Van Winkle, Rumpelstiltskin* are stronger titles than *Cinderella, Heidi, Little Women* and the *Sleeping*

Beauty." In addition Miss Spencer gives this sage advice: "Open and close the season with a strong title, and place experimental, lesser-known titles in between."

Certain titles seem to possess hidden charm. The very names suggest mystery, intrigue, conflict, or romance. A few play titles will serve to illustrate: *Death Takes a Holiday, Beyond the Horizon, The Devil's Disciple, If I Were King, School for Scandal, Of Thee I Sing, Dead End, Ah, Wilderness!, A Streetcar Named Desire, The Green Pastures,* and *Abie's Irish Rose* are all titles that catch the fancy. What's in a name? Plenty!

Dr. George W. Crane reported an almost unbelievable study of the comparative public interest in two different sets of book titles for exactly the same books. Each of the titles was given the same advertising and promotion over a specified period of time. All factors were the same except that the titles were changed. The results from the report are so amazing that they sound like "Believe It or Not." Notice the following ten comparisons of the number of books sold under one title as compared with another title:

The King Enjoys Himself	8,000
The Lustful King Enjoys Himself	38,000
Pen, Pencil, and Poison	5,000
The Story of a Notorious Criminal	15,000
The Truth About Patent Medicine	10,000
Patent Medicine and the Public Health	3,000
The Art of Controversy	100
How to Argue Logically	30,000
The Art of Courtship	17,500
The Art of Kissing	60,500
An Introduction to Einstein	15,000
Einstein's Theory of Relativity Explained	4,000
Nietzsche: Who He Was and What He Stood For	19,000
The Story of Nietzsche's Philosophy	45,000
Quest For a Blonde Mistress	50,000
Fleece of Gold	6,000

Markheim's Murder	7,000
Markheim	100
The Mystery of the Iron Mask	11,000
The Mystery of the Man in the Iron Mask	30,000

6. *Variety is the spice of life.* A season of the same kind of plays is like a diet of the same food. All cake, all pie, or all meat soon becomes monotonous. Then, too, different people have different tastes, and there must be something enjoyable for all. Sometimes a few selfish people in high places select only what they themselves want, and disregard the public completely. Such selfishness is not only unfair, it is dangerous. It has emptied many theatres. It will empty yours.

Take a look at the various types of drama: satire, English comedy, rural comedy, low comedy, sophisticated comedy, mystery, drama, and tragedy. For a healthy, balanced program there must be something of interest and variety for all.

7. *A well-known author is always an asset.* William Shakespeare is still the best box-office draw even after three hundred years. Leading university theatres in America report that their most successful plays include *Macbeth, Julius Caesar, Hamlet, King Lear, Taming of the Shrew, Midsummer Night's Dream, As You Like It, Comedy of Errors,* and *Twelfth Night.* This fact should offer encouragement and give vigor to community, college, and even high-school theatres. Besides Shakespeare, the names of Shaw, O'Neill, Maxwell Anderson, Ibsen, Chekhov, Kingsley, Cohan, Hart, as well as other eminent playwrights, give support and dignity to the list of theatre offerings.

8. *There can be no substitute for quality in play selection.* With the great wealth of dramatic literature available from the ancient past to the present, there is no excuse for dealing with theatrical trash. People who go to a theatre are entitled to something worthwhile. Whether the play is light comedy or heavy tragedy, it should bear the mark of quality.

9. *Timeliness can supply a fitness which may not otherwise exist.* Obversely, a great drama may lose favor as the current of social, economic, and political events change direction. The rise of a play's popularity can

be surprisingly sudden. Plays concerned with politics, wars, elections, and reforms may gain and lose popularity within a span of weeks or even days. For example, *Flight to the West* was a good play on December 6, 1941, but a day later, December 7, it was a museum piece; Pearl Harbor cruelly dated it. Years later it made a partial recovery. Some directors and promoters seem to have a sixth sense for choosing a timely play. More often it is stock-market luck.

10. Avoid the hurried decision. The importance of thorough study with an open mind for selecting the right play can hardly be overstressed. Very few theatres could be charged with too much deliberation on this initial step. Choosing a play is too vital to be left to the chance expressed in doggerel parody of a familiar rhyme:

> Eenie, meenie, miney, mon
> Grab a play and put it on.
> If it fails and makes you sad,
> Grab another just as bad.

11. Keep the objectives in mind. One eminent producer gave this word of caution, "We have found through experience that the average audience have worries and problems of their own and they seem to prefer entertainment which permits them to relax. Hence we use tragedy sparingly in our theatre. We believe also that it is the business of the churches to preach and do good; the business of the theatre is to entertain."

12. Permissions and royalties should be properly cleared. As soon as the play selections are approved by the theatre, all questions of royalties, permissions, and scripts should be cleared with the publisher or controller. This should be done before any public announcements are made. In both the United States and Great Britain, many plays currently staged are copyrighted. A copyright gives exclusive ownership to a literary work. The term of copyright in the United States is twenty-eight years with a right of renewal for another twenty-eight years, or a total of fifty-six years. Most successful playwrights do not pass up the renewal privilege. However, a number of popular plays are now available without royalty because they have passed the fifty-six years of protections. For example, the following well-known plays by George Bernard Shaw carried high royalties, but are now in public domain in the United States: *Arms and the Man, Candida, Man of Destiny, You Never Can Tell, The Devil's Disciple, Mrs. Warren's Profession, The Philanderer,* and *Man and Superman.* If you are in doubt as to whether or not a play is free, check its publication dates at the public library, or better still, inquire from some major play publisher.

Royalty quotations listed in catalogues are usually maximum for one performance; the rate for more than one is generally lower. Some publishers establish a royalty charge on a percentage of the theatre's gross sales. In other cases the purchase of so many scripts or copies of the play is the only royalty assessment. The most commonly quoted fee is a flat rate of so many dollars for a performance or group of performances.

The proper procedure is to write a letter to the publisher asking for permission and a statement of royalty. The following data should be submitted in your letter: (1) name of organization, (2) dates of production, (3) size of the theatre, (4) size of the community, (5) admission prices to be charged.

It is regrettable that some institutions, including churches and schools, have considered it perfectly ethical and legal to evade payment of royalties by such devious methods as keeping things quiet, changing the name of the play, and even changing the names of the players. Failure to realize that such evasions are in violation of the federal copyright law may eventually embarrass the offenders. A worthy cause is not sufficient reason to request that an author waive his rights to his property. Bernard Shaw, when asked to waive the fee on one of his plays to be given for the benefit of an old ladies' home said, "If you can't take care of your old ladies, why should I?" No theatre or play-producing group can afford to operate on the theory that evasions of royalty are all right if one is clever enough to get by with them. The same groups that would evade payment of royalties would probably not approve of people sneaking into the theatre without paying for their tickets.

13. Check these ten questions on play selection. If you can answer them with a "yes," you have very likely chosen the right play. If not, it will pay to search further before announcing a final decision. It is not uncommon for an amateur theatre to send out a notice announcing a change of play for some lame excuse such as, "We could not cast it with the people we have available." Your patrons will be more interested in getting what they paid for than in hearing about your problems. A change of play for even the best reason weakens the theatre prestige.

———1. Will our audience enjoy it?

———2. Will we be proud to present it?

———3. Will it give satisfaction to all concerned?

———4. Will it come within our budget, i.e., can we afford it?

———5. Can we cast it successfully with our people?

———6. Can we stage it expeditiously?

———7. Are we equipped to handle the scenery and lighting problems?

———8. Can we costume it?

———9. Is it worthwhile theatre?

———10. Will it help to build our future productions?

II

HOW TO PLAN A BUDGET

> When duty comes a knocking at your gate,
> Welcome him in. For if you bid him wait,
> He will depart and then return once more
> And bring seven other duties to your door.
> Edwin Markham

In the hard, everyday business world, theatre people are too often regarded as impractical in both personal and professional life. There is some implication that practicality and artistry are incompatible. It is believed that theatre people generally are incapable of adjusting their spending to suit their earnings. Whether or not this reputation of business incompetence is deserving has long been a moot question. Without further reference to it, one may admit that there is plenty of room for improvement.

That those truly interested in show business should pay more attention to its commonly neglected financial aspect is fully attested by the plight of the professional theatre today. With the advent of television, thousands of theatre ventures over the nation are having additional worries. Some have failed not because they have poor products, not because theatre is outmoded, but because important phases of business management, public relations, and promotion are neglected. Competition is too keen. Although many legitimate theatres have long been folded and forgotten, it is likely that the mistakes and pitfalls can be avoided if theatre people of today are willing to open their eyes to what has happened and to face the facts. Facts are hard things to face.

It is amazing to find that such a vital step as planning even a simple budget is often neglected. Many problems could be simplified and many misunderstandings and miscalculations avoided if, at the outset, sufficient care and time were given to this important task.

Just four simple words can express the only two known methods of balancing a budget:

1. INCREASE RECEIPTS
2. REDUCE SPENDING

A theatre budget, like a bank account, ought to show a comfortable balance. This balance is much more likely to exist if there is a well-made plan. Guessing and hoping cannot be written into the budget; there must be realism.

Making a budget may not be fun and it may not be easy, but it is an early duty of top priority. Clear it out of the way, for it cannot wait.

The first step in actual preparation of a theatre budget is to make an estimate of total income from all sources. It is well to have this estimate somewhat on the conservative side. Sources of income vary, but here are the five most common:

1. Ticket sales
2. Flat fees paid for a production
3. Advertising in the printed program
4. Gifts and contributions
5. Miscellaneous, which might include concessions, interest, sale of property, television rights, etc.

It is altogether possible that a theatre may overlook entirely an opportunity to pick up an important item of income which it could just as well have. If such an inclusion could add even 2 per cent it might mean the difference between success or failure. The margin of difference between failure and success may be small, but it is important.

The second step is to decide on how the total income is to be allocated. An easy and simple approach is to prepare the first draft in percentages. This gives an idea of proportional distribution. For example, you start with 100 per cent and tentatively assign a given per cent to each item on the budget. The percentage approach will give a sense of proportion and clearer perspective so that budget-makers will not cut one item and overspend on another. It often happens that some ridiculously large sum goes for costumes or lighting, while the advertising nourishment is reduced to a point where the production dies a horrible death in the box office. Every budget item is important and must be treated with fairness.

A representative from each department should participate in budget-making. It should never be a one-man job.

With the general layout given in percentages, it is simple arithmetic to multiply the per cent for a given item by the estimated total budget. For example, if the total budget is $10,000 and 11 per cent is assigned to advertising, it means you have a maximum of $1,100 to cover all costs of advertising. If the budget is $1,000, you have $110 for that item. If the entire amount set up for advertising is not needed, the unspent part should remain in the budget. But what might happen is that some ambitious department, finding out about the saving, may seek to pick it up. Remember the Tenth Commandment: "Thou shalt not covet. . . ." The head of a department who operates on the theory that he can overspend because someone else will surely economize is a luxury which no theatre can afford. Such dishonesty creates ill will and should not be permitted—not even once.

Simply because percentages have been set up does not mean that the budget is inflexible. When the plays have been selected, there may be need for redistribution. However, the total money available must not be exceeded—careful budgeting might reduce it. If one item is to be increased by twenty-five dollars, some other item or items must be reduced by twenty-five dollars. When such simple things are set down on paper, they seem obvious, but in theatre budgets, as in other things, the most obvious is hard to see. "The owl, looking at the sun, cries out, 'Where is it?'"

In the process of working up a theatre budget, these two annoying questions always come up:

1. How can you prepare a budget before you know what plays you are going to do?

2. How can you select the plays before you know what the budget is going to allow?

The answer is that the two problems have to be solved simultaneously, step by step, to avoid the argument, "Which comes first, the play or the budget?"

On the pages immediately following are two examples of beginning budget layouts. The "First Budget" is worked on an anticipated income of ten thousand dollars before the names of the plays are definite. The "Second Budget" shows the redistribution of the ten thousand dollars when the names of the plays are known, including their special requirements, travel, and so on. Although many items are revised, the total estimated income available remains practically the same.

Because no two situations are identical, no two budgets are alike. The local scene must determine many things. For example, some groups have no "rental of theatre" item; in others the "rental of theatre" may range anywhere from ten dollars to five hundred dollars. Always the budget must be studied carefully, with attention to the local situation.

A sample budget on the production costs of *The Glass Menagerie* compiled by David Heilwell has been released by the American National Theatre and Academy. This budget shows how nine different groups producing the same play incurred expenses which ranged from $900 for a college to $65,000 for the New York production. One college group spent $5 for costumes; the New York production spent $2,000. The nine groups reporting are well known, and it is likely that they all had acceptable productions. Some theatre directors can produce a play with little expense, whereas others feel that they must operate on the grand scale. Fortunately, the cost of a production is not an index to its popularity or success.

FIRST BUDGET — EARLY PLANNING (BEFORE PLAYS ARE CHOSEN)

Expense Items	%	Total Amounts	Play A	Play B	Play C	Play D
1. Staff Salaries	19	$ 1,900	$ 475	$ 475	$ 475	$ 475
2. Scenery	10	1,000	250	250	250	250
3. Lighting	2	200	50	50	50	50
4. Properties	3	300	75	75	75	75
5. Costumes	8	800	200	200	200	200
6. Musicians, Music	4	400	100	100	100	100
7. Scripts	1	100	25	25	25	25
8. Royalties	6	600	150	150	150	150
9. Advertising & Publicity	10	1,000	250	250	250	250
10. Box Office	4	400	100	100	100	100
11. Programs	3	300	75	75	75	75
12. Tickets	2	200	50	50	50	50
13. Taxes (State)	2	200	50	50	50	50
14. Rental of Theatres	5	500	125	125	125	125
15. Reserve Fund	15	1,500	375	375	375	375
16. Miscellaneous	6	600	150	150	150	150
TOTAL EXPENSE	100%	$10,000	$2,500	$2,500	$2,500	$2,500

FIG. 1.

FIG. 2.

SECOND BUDGET – AFTER PLAYS ARE CHOSEN

Expense Items	%	Total Amounts	Hit Comedy	Mystery	Classic	Musical	Reductions	Additions
1. Staff Salaries	19	$1,900	$ 475.00	$ 475.00	$ 475.00	$ 475.00		
* 2. Scenery	10	1,000	150.00	100.00	250.00	500.00	$250	$250
3. Lighting	2	200	50.00	50.00	50.00	50.00		
* 4. Properties	3¼	325	75.00	75.00	100.00	75.00		25
* 5. Costumes	7¾	775	57.50	57.50	292.50	367.50	285	260
* 6. Musicians, Music	3	300			100.00	200.00	100	
* 7. Scripts	2	200	25.00	25.00	25.00	125.00		100
* 8. Royalties	4½	450	150.00	150.00		150.00	150	
9. Advertising & Publicity	10	1,000	250.00	250.00	250.00	250.00		
10. Box Office	4	400	100.00	100.00	100.00	100.00		
11. Programs	3	300	75.00	75.00	75.00	75.00		
12. Tickets	2	200	50.00	50.00	50.00	50.00		
13. Taxes (State)	2	200	50.00	50.00	50.00	50.00		
14. Rental of Theatres	5	500	125.00	125.00	125.00	125.00		
15. Reserve Fund	15	1,500	375.00	375.00	375.00	375.00		
16. Miscellaneous	6	600	150.00	150.00	150.00	150.00		
TOTAL EXPENSE	98½%	$9,850	$2,157.50	$2,107.50	$2,467.50	$3,117.50	$785	$635

* Revised items. In reworking the "Second Budget" there was a savings of 1½% or $150.00.

III

SELECTING THE BEST DATES

Choosing the right dates for your productions is just as important as choosing the right play. Selecting the wrong date can cause failure even though there are careful preparations and thorough promotion. In one instance, a theatre overlooked the fact that November 4 was the presidential election date and played to an empty house. Another theatre reported having scheduled a play during Holy Week, which brought forth storms of protest. Such errors are countless. The Federal Income Tax lowers the boom the week of April 15, a period almost as unpleasant as the "Ides of March" in Julius Caesar's time.

If the manager and the director would only sit down with the year's calendar in front of them and mark the national and local dates to be avoided, they could save themselves needless headaches. There are plenty of problems to solve without dealing in date complications and conflicts which could have been foreseen and solved. Anyone can think about the date when it comes close. Why not think about this problem while there is still time to avoid a collision?

Methodical Approaches to Date Selection

1. Consider your competition. Can you keep away from other big events? If your theatre is important enough that you can ask other productions to keep off your scheduled dates, you're a wheel. If this is not the case, then you must adjust. "If the mountain will not come to Mohammed, then Mohammed must go to the mountain." In some localities sports events, such as basketball, football, baseball, or hockey, reign supreme and to clash with them is stupidity. The local picture must be considered with caution. To schedule a performance in competition with events which involve community-wide participation is fatal unless some reciprocal business tie-in can be arranged. If such collaboration is possible, the date conflict may be turned to your financial advantage. However, the tie-in should be made well in advance and all plans and commitments must be specific and definite.

Find out what is coming your way. Will there be any regional or state conventions or conferences sponsored by churches or educational groups? What is planned by service clubs such as Lions, Rotary, Kiwanis, Exchange, and others? For example, a regional dental convention was scheduled a week before a college theatre was presenting an interesting comedy. The theatre management met with the program committee of the dental association and arranged to present a special performance for the convention guests. The theatre realized a good profit and the dental association was thoroughly delighted. Such opportunities are common, and a manager who is fully awake will find them. The mouse just happened to be coming out of the hole, but it wasn't just by chance that the cat was there. Alert management will capitalize on special events if possible. Every state has a strong educational association with annual meetings involving thousands of teachers. That could be important. Be circumspect. You must see around corners.

If there is a regular schedule of big name dramatic productions on television, they should be avoided if possible. Anything and everything that can be done to avoid conflicts will be appreciated by your patrons.

In most cities it is unwise to attempt competition with a firstrate road show, symphony, or ballet. If you can see a conflict coming, avoid it. Sometimes you cannot see it, but more often you can, and looking ahead beats the "hope and pray" technique.

As a practical solution to the vexing problems of competition, concert and theatre managers in numerous cities have actually organized a council where all dates are cleared. Such an organization can offer mutual support instead of the common practice of bumping heads. If you do not have a clearing house, you will find it to your advantage to take the initiative and organize one. The idea of meeting on a friendly basis with your competitors can be a benefit to all.

It is not enough that the day of the show itself be free from conflict; two similar events booked closely together can damage each other. Recently in an average American city the Royal (Sadler's Wells) Ballet

Every month has Theatre Days. Mark them, use them. Here is February example.

FEBRUARY 1961

S	M	T	W	T	F	S
			1	2	3	4
5	6	⑦	⑧	9	10	⑪
⑫	13	⑭	15	16	17	18
19	⑳	21	㉒	23	24	25
26	㉗	28				

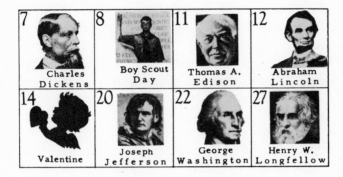

7 Charles Dickens	8 Boy Scout Day	11 Thomas A. Edison	12 Abraham Lincoln
14 Valentine	20 Joseph Jefferson	22 George Washington	27 Henry W. Longfellow

What excitement February offers! Romance, invention, statesmanship, poetry, and theatre. There are more than twenty-five plays about Washington; a similar number about Lincoln.

George Washington Slept Here — Kaufman & Hart
Valley Forge — Maxwell Anderson
Washington Marches On — Oliver Price

Abe Lincoln in Illinois — R. E. Sherwood
If Booth Had Missed — Arthur Goodman
Prologue to Glory — E. P. Conkle

There is rich material in Dickens' *Oliver Twist*, *Christmas Carol*, and *A Tale Of Two Cities*.

Valentine's Day offers infinite possibilities. And Joseph Jefferson's birthday would be ideal for a revival of *Rip Van Winkle*. For three generations Jefferson made Rip the most talked of character on the American stage.

The use of holidays will get extra publicity too.

FIG. 3.

was scheduled within a week of the Ballet Theatre. Although either one would have been a sellout, both suffered financially.

2. *Avoid holidays of the year.* Unless events have a special connection with, or appropriateness to, a holiday these dates should be avoided. *The Messiah,* for example, is traditionally popular at Christmas time. Some religious plays, such as *The Vigil* and *The Family Portrait,* are appropriate at Easter or Christmas time. But ordinarily holidays are dangerous.

The month of December, with the possible exception of the first week, is not a good time to sell entertainment because of the tremendous emphasis placed on Christmas buying. People's minds are so besieged with slogans, such as "Only 15 more shopping days until Christmas," that everything else takes a second place. One must meet the situation realistically. The extent to which people will exhaust themselves financially and physically is hard to explain. Because of this tremendous emphasis, the period including the month of December and the first half of January is not a good time for theatre business. Many of the commercial theatres take annual vacations around Christmas time, but there are exceptions. For example, it has been found that the week between Christmas and New Year's is an excellent time for show business in many localities. The *Nutcracker Ballet* with Tschaikowsky's famous music has been a box-office success in many cities during the week after Christmas.

3. *Watch the month and the week.* Pay days usually fall on the first and the fifteenth or the tenth and the twenty-fifth of the month. Other things being equal, you would do well to schedule your entertainment right after pay day. People are always more apt to spend money when they have a little extra on hand. When money becomes scarce Americans cut their amusement budget as the first economy. In a booming economy entertainment is in big demand and people are willing to pay good prices for it; but in a retrenching economy entertainment budgets are the first to suffer. The idea of "feeding the soul" as expressed by the Persian poet, Sa'di, may be an oriental or European concept, but it's not in the hearts of the American audience.

> If of thy mortal goods thou art bereft,
> And of thy slender store two loaves alone to thee are left,
> Sell one and with the dole
> Buy hyacinths to feed thy soul.

IMPORTANT DAYS AND HOLIDAYS

January
   1—New Year's Day
      First part of month generally
      poor time. People are recu-
      perating from Christmas hol-
      idays.

May
      May suggests lighter enter-
      tainment.
      Spring tonic is in order.
   1—May Day
      —Mother's Day (2nd Sunday)
   30—Memorial Day in 42 states

February
      A good entertainment month.
   12—Lincoln's Birthday in most
      states.
   14—Valentine's Day
   22—Washington's Birthday

June
      June is a doubtful month
   14—Flag Day
      —Father's Day (3rd Sunday)

March
      Generally a good month for
      all show business.
   17—St. Patrick's Day

July
      Excellent month for outdoor
      shows.
   4—Independence Day

April
      Note observance of Lent be-
      fore Easter. Give at least six
      weeks advance planning to
      any April dates.
   1—April Fool's Day
      —Good Friday
      —Easter
   15—Income Tax deadline

August
      Success depends upon thor-
      ough promotion, although
      there are no holidays.

NOTE: Add to the above, all important local dates such as major competitive en-
      tertainment, special celebrations, conventions, big athletic events, and state
      holidays. Dates following pay days are to be chosen over those farther away
      from pay day.

September

> School begins in early September: this may be a conflict. Latter part of month is better.
> —Labor Day (1st Monday)

November

> Avoid election dates.
> —Elections (1st Tuesday after 1st Monday)
> Some state elections do not fall on this date, but the majority do.
> 11—Veterans' Day in most states
> —Thanksgiving (Last Thursday)

October

> A good month all the way.
> 12—Columbus Day in most states
> 31—Hallowe'en

December

> Only the first week of December is good. Avoid the rest unless the event has special significance.
> 25—Christmas Day

STATE HOLIDAYS

Besides national holidays, most states also observe dates of special significance.

Alabama

Jan.	19	Birthday of Robert E. Lee
Apr.	13	Birthday of Thomas Jefferson
Apr.	26	Confederate Memorial Day
June	3	Birthday of Jefferson Davis
Shrove Tues.—Mardi Gras		

Alaska

Mar.	30	Seward Day
June	30	Admission Day
Oct.	18	Alaska Day

Arizona

Feb.	14	Admission Day

Arkansas

Jan.	19	Birthday of Robert E. Lee
June	3	Birthday of Jefferson Davis

California

Mar.	7	Arbor Day
Sept.	9	Admission Day

Colorado

Aug.	1	Colorado Day

Connecticut
> No state holidays

Delaware
Dec. 7 Delaware Day

District of Columbia
Jan. 20 Inauguration Day, every
          4 years

Florida
Jan. 19 Birthday of Robert E.
          Lee
Apr. 26 Confederate Memorial
          Day
June 3   Birthday of Jefferson
          Davis
Oct. 12 Farmer's Day
Shrove Tues—Mardi Gras (in some
          towns)

Georgia
Jan. 19 Birthday of Robert E.
          Lee
Feb. 12 Georgia Day
Apr. 26 Confederate Memorial
          Day
June 3   Birthday of Jefferson
          Davis

Hawaii
Mar. 28 Kuhio Day
June 11 Kamehameha Day
Aug. 21 Admission Day

Idaho
June 15 Pioneer Day

Illinois
> No state holidays

Indiana
> No state holidays

Iowa
> No state holidays

Kansas
> No state holidays

Kentucky
Jan. 19 Birthday of Robert E.
          Lee
Jan. 30 Birthday of Franklin D.
          Roosevelt
June 3   Confederate Memorial
          Day

Louisiana
Jan. 8   Battle of New Orleans,
          or Jackson Day
Jan. 19 Birthday of Robert E.
          Lee
June 3   Confederate Memorial
          Day
          Birthday of Jefferson
          Davis
Aug. 30 Birthday of Huey P.
          Long
Shrove Tues.—Mardi Gras (in some
          parishes)

Maine
Apr. 19 Patriot's Day

Maryland
Mar. 25   Maryland Day
Sept. 12   Defender's Day

Massachusetts
Apr. 19   Patriot's Day
June 17   Bunker Hill Day

Michigan
Aug. 14   Victory Day

Minnesota
            No state holidays

Mississippi
Jan. 19   Birthday of Robert E.
            Lee
Apr. 26   Confederate   Memorial
            Day
June 3   Birthday   of   Jefferson
            Davis

Missouri
Oct.   1   Missouri Day

Montana
            No state holidays
Nebraska
Apr. 22   Arbor Day

Nevada
Oct. 31   Admission Day

New Hampshire
            No state holidays

New Jersey
            No state holidays

New Mexico
            No state holidays

New York
            No state holidays

North Carolina
Jan. 19   Birthday   of   Robert   E.
            Lee
Apr. 12   Halifax   Independence
            Day
May 10   Confederate   Memorial
            Day
May 20   Anniversary of the sign-
            ing of the Mecklenberg
            Declaration of Indepen-
            dence

North Dakota
            No state holidays

Ohio
            No state holidays

Oklahoma
Apr. 22   Opening   of   Oklahoma
            Territory
Nov.   4   Will Rogers Day

Oregon
            No state holidays

Pennsylvania
June 14   Flag Day
Oct. 24   Pennsylvania Day

Rhode Island
            No state holidays

South Carolina

Jan. 19   Birthday of Robert E. Lee

May 10   Confederate Memorial Day

June 3   Birthday of Jefferson Davis

Dec. 28   Birthday of Woodrow Wilson

South Dakota

No state holidays

Tennessee

Jan. 19   Birthday of Robert E. Lee

Mar. 15   Birthday of Andrew Jackson

June 3   Confederate Memorial Day

July 13   Birthday of General Nathan Bedford Forrest

Texas

Jan. 19   Birthday of Robert E. Lee

Mar. 2   Independence Day

Apr. 21   San Jacinto Day

June 3   Birthday of Jefferson Davis

Utah

July 24   Pioneer Day

Vermont

Aug. 16   Battle of Bennington Day

Virginia

Jan. 19   Birthday of Robert E. Lee

Apr. 13   Birthday of Thomas Jefferson

June 3   Birthday of Jefferson Davis

Washington

No state holidays

West Virginia

June 20   West Virginia Day

Wisconsin

No state holidays

Wyoming

No state holidays

Many cities have holidays, special days of their own which are not recognized in the rest of the state. For example, New Orleans has a Spring Festival and the Mardi Gras, both so city-wide that any other entertainment would have to conform. While other cities may not have programs of such magnitude, it is good policy to consult the calendar before making up your program.

Days of the week have different values. After long and careful study, movie theatre managers have made a point evaluation of the seven days. On the basis of ten points for the entire week, they evaluated them as follows: Monday 1, Tuesday 1, Wednesday 1, Thursday 1, Friday 1, Saturday 3, and Sunday 2. This scale varies in different states and cities, but the pattern runs somewhat the same for all amusements, with the exception that Friday is often as good as Saturday. As a general rule the heavy demand for tickets falls on the week end.

4. *Weather is a vital factor in your scheduling*. It must be studied locally. Heavy rains or snows, extreme cold or heat can be death for the box office. Midwinter in the Rocky Mountain area may spell "snowbound." Long and heavy rains in other areas are just as devastating. Although no one has been able to predict the weather accurately, any local forecaster can advise you concerning most likely inclement periods. The following poem gives an idea about what people generally expect from the weather:

> January brings the snow,
> Makes our feet and fingers glow.
> February brings the rain,
> Thaws the frozen earth again.
> March brings breezes loud and shrill
> To stir the dancing daffodil.
> April brings the primrose sweet,
> Scatters daisies at our feet.
> May brings flocks of pretty lambs
> Skipping by their fleecy dams.
> June brings tulips, lilies, roses,
> Fills the children's hands with posies.
> Hot July brings cooling showers,
> Apricots and gillyflowers.
> August brings sheaves of corn,
> Then the harvest home is borne.
> Warm September brings the fruit;
> Sportsmen then begin to shoot.
> Fresh October brings the pheasant;
> Then to gather nuts is pleasant.

> Dull November brings the blast;
> Then the leaves are whirling fast.
> Chill December brings the sleet,
> Blazing fire and Christmas treat.

5. *Alert theatre managements will plan production dates a year in advance if possible.* The next step is to see that a list of those dates is made public. All groups that might be considered competitive should receive a copy of the theatre's schedule. They will not wish to be blamed for a conflict. Most conflicts are due to lack of advance information. It is an excellent idea to supply the newspapers with a handy little calendar which includes all available data. Newspapers are always willing and helpful in advising groups as to what is going on when; it is part of their business.

Not only should the theatre see that other groups have a copy of their schedule, but it should keep a copy of what other groups are doing. The best and most obvious value of such alertness is that theatre publicity is funneled into all organizations planning activities. Such leadership and service creates good will, good understanding, and good business.

Our month of January comes from Janus, the ancient Roman god of the gates and doors; he was also god of all beginnings. Janus is represented as having two faces so that he could see the future as well as the past. Descendants of Janus in the theatre are not many, but there are a few. These few know that it is important to get a calendar in front of them and study it as they plan ahead.

The calendar below shows certain warning signals:

There are a few theatres which plan their programs not one year but several years in advance. Some theatre people will respond to this idea as does the old lady in *The Royal Family,* who, on being told that some families actually all sit down around the table together and eat their meals, replies in astonishment, "How quaint."

SHAKESPEARE

Ashland, Oregon

July 24 through September 3, 1961

1961	JULY-AUGUST-SEPTEMBER				1961	
SUN	MON	TUES	WED	THUR	FRI	SAT
	July **24** MND	July **25** HAM	July **26** AW	July **27** H IV	July **28** MND	July **29** HAM
July **30** AW	July **31** H IV	Aug **1** MND	Aug **2** HAM	Aug **3** AW	Aug **4** H IV	Aug **5** MND
Aug **6** HAM	Aug **7** AW	Aug **8** H IV	Aug **9** MND	Aug **10** HAM	Aug **11** AW	Aug **12** H IV
Aug **13** MND	Aug **14** HAM	Aug **15** AW	Aug **16** H IV	Aug **17** MND	Aug **18** HAM	Aug **19** AW
Aug **20** H IV	Aug **21** ALC	Aug **22** MND	Aug **23** HAM	Aug **24** AW	Aug **25** H IV	Aug **26** ALC
Aug **27** MND	Aug **28** HAM	Aug **29** AW	Aug **30** H IV	Aug **31** ALC	Sept **1** MND	Sept **2** HAM
Sept **3** AW	A Midsummer Night's Dream All's Well That Ends Well" "The Alchemist"				"Hamlet" "Henry IV, Part I"	

FIG. 4.

The Oregon Shakespearean Festival prepares the above calendar to give names of plays and dates even though the plays change every night. It is simple, complete, and easy to understand. Be Calendarwise.

IV

ORDERING TICKETS FOR THE BOX OFFICE

Before sending off the final order for the precious little pasteboards known as theatre tickets, there are four short but important questions which should be answered. According to ticket printers, the answers to the questions are too often incomplete or incorrect and such errors are certain to cause delay and expense.

These are the questions: *When? Where? How? What?*

When to Order Tickets

As soon as events and dates are established authentically, the ticket order should be placed. A qualified printer will require one to two weeks, depending on the size and complexity of the request. When the order is sent in, it is wise to get a statement from the printer as to when it will be shipped; otherwise the theatre manager may have one delivery date in mind and the printer another. The shipment may require a few days to reach you after it leaves the printer. Shipping time will, of course, not be a consideration in large cities where there are ticket printers. Finally, the box office must have time to check the tickets for accuracy and rack them properly. All this means that there should be at least a month from the date of order until the tickets are ready for sale to the public.

Many theatres are guilty of procrastination in this vital duty of ticket ordering. As the opening show date approaches there is panic, while the job that should have been done with care and attention for details is hurried through under pressure.

Where to Order Tickets

The experienced theatre manager selects a qualified ticket printer who understands the many little problems involved in this type of work.

Such a printer knows exactly what should be on the ticket, and if any information has been omitted he will call it to your attention rather than printing the order of tickets incorrectly. It is easy, in making up an order, to overlook an item such as tax or some other small detail, but the expert's double check will pick it up in almost every case.

Although some custom printers may be able to do an acceptable job of ticket printing most of them find the work too complicated and involved. It is a job requiring special machinery and know-how.

The right kind of ticket, properly printed and placed on sale, will help dignify the theatre that sells it. The box office personnel need not worry about ticket errors, which may cause confusion and embarrassment.

Any of the following ticket printers should be willing to help you prepare your order and give practical suggestions. Upon request, they will send samples and prices. If you send a seating plan of your theatre, the printer will furnish reserved seat tickets according to specifications. Once a printer has your seating plan on file, he can use it for future orders. The following are reliable and economical sources for theatre tickets of all kinds:

Acme Ticket Co.
Colorado Springs
Colorado

American Ticket Co.
513-515 Greene Ave.
Brooklyn, New York

American Ticket Corp.
3153 W. 36th Street
Chicago, Illinois

Ansell-Simplex Ticket Co.
2834-50 W. Chicago Ave.
Chicago 22, Illinois

Arcus Ticket Co.
348 N. Ashland Ave.
Chicago, Illinois

Daly Ticket Co.
506 Vandalia St.
Collinsville, Illinois

Elliott Ticket Co.
409 Lafayette St.
New York 3, New York

Fair Publishing House
P.O. Box 350
Norwalk, Ohio

Globe Ticket Co.
with 8 offices at:
   420 South San Pedro St.
   Los Angeles, California

   861 Lee Street SW
   Atlanta, Georgia

1020 South Wabash
Chicago, Illinois

620 Commonwealth Avenue
Boston, Massachusetts

SW 706 Chestnut Street
St. Louis, Missouri

160 W. 14th Street
New York, New York

112 N. 12th Street
Philadelphia, Pennsylvania

6002 McKinley
Tacoma, Washington

Hancock Bros., Inc.
1900 Carroll Ave.
San Francisco 24, California

H. S. Crocker Co., Inc.
1000 San Mateo Ave.
San Bruno, California

International Ticket Co.
50 Grafton Ave.
Newark 4, New Jersey

Linopress Company
2132 Harbor Blvd.
Costa Mesa, California

McGill-Warner Co.
215 E. 9th Street
St. Paul 1, Minnesota

National Ticket Co.
Shamokin
Pennsylvania

Premier Southern Ticket Co.
1621 Dana Ave.
Cincinnati 7, Ohio

Toledo Ticket Co.
3963 Catawba St.
Toledo, Ohio

Weldon, Williams & Lick
Fort Smith
Arkansas

How to Order Tickets

If you have not already selected a ticket printer, it would be a good idea to consult two or more printers before making a decision. Other things being equal, some consideration should be given to distances from your theatre to the printer. Time for communications and shipments may be important.

In order for the ticket company to give its best service, you should supply the following data: (1) Seating capacity of theatre or auditorium. (2) Number and arrangement of seats on the main floor, loges, and balcony. (3) Number of performances for which tickets will be printed at one time. (4) Distribution of prices; when the price changes the ticket color should also change. (5) Size of ticket you intend to use (there are two standard sizes: 1¼" × 4" and 1½" × 3½"). It will be helpful to include also a detailed reproduction of the seating plan which shows the number of rows, the number of seats in each row, the sections and aisles. The following type of letter may be helpful:

Kingsbury Hall, University of Utah
University Theatre of Utah

Phone EM 3-2033   Salt Lake City 12, Utah

August 2, 1970

Globe Ticket Company
420 South San Pedro Street
Los Angeles 13, California

Gentlemen:

This is our order for reserved seat tickets for 1970 - 71. Enclosed is the seating plan of Kingsbury Hall.

We need a season-strip ticket for six productions. Tickets should have a "season audit stub" and a "single audit stub." Each ticket should show the breakdown of both season and single sales. Tickets will be 1½ x 3½ inches plus the single audit stub which adds a half inch, making a total of four inches.

The following information should be on the tickets:

(at top)   University Theatre   1970–71
                    Kingsbury Hall ———— Eve. at 8:15 P.M.
                 $5.00 $7.50

Season Price		Single Price		Season Price		Single Price	
Est. Pr.	.815	Est. Pr.	.98	Est. Pr.	1.225	Est. Pr.	1.47
St. Tax	.020	St. Tax	.02	St. Tax	.025	St. Tax	.03
	$.835		$1.00		$1.25		$1.50

Each show plays five performances: Tuesday thru Saturday.

BUS STOP	Oct. 6, 7, 8, 9, 10 '70	KIND LADY	Feb. 7, 8, 9, 10, 11 '71
THE BAT	Nov. 1, 2, 3, 4, 5 '70	LILIOM	Mar. 2, 3, 4, 5, 6 '71
HAMLET	Dec. 3, 4, 5, 6, 7 '70	OUR TOWN	Apr. 3, 4, 5, 6, 7 '71

Please ship the tickets prepaid and add the shipping charges to the bill. We must have these tickets no later than September 7, 1970.

Sincerely yours,

What Types of Tickets to Use

In order to determine the kind of ticket which best suits the show manager's use, it is well to take a look at the various kinds available. Although there are a number of variations in size, shape, and color, the general types of tickets are as described below. Illustrations of them are shown on pages 34 and 37.

1. Season tickets with audit stubs. Many successful university and community theatres now use season tickets with reserved seats for each show. For example, a theatre sells a package of five shows to Mr. Doe at a special season price of $5. Mr. Doe will receive five tickets, either stapled together in a little pad or in a perforated sheet so that the tickets can be easily detached as they are used. Which one is used makes little difference; both are convenient and serve the same purpose. The pad is a little more expensive to prepare because the printer has to assemble and staple the tickets in the right order with the first one on top.

The five tickets for the productions are all for the same seats and the night of the week. For example, they may be all for Tuesdays, or all for Wednesdays, Thursdays, and so on. They would not be mixed as to nights. They are alike accept for the name of the show and the date. As the season tickets are sold, each one should be stamped "SEASON" in large bold letters. It is suggested that the size of the letters on this stamp be about one half inch high and about two inches long. There should be sufficient ink on the stamp-pad for a clear impression.

With each set of tickets there is a season audit stub, which is detached and kept by the box office when the sale is made. It is the same size as the tickets and has the same seat numbers. There is a space with lines on which to write the name, address, and telephone number of the patron. These audit stubs serve four functions: (1) They are a double check or audit on the money received. (2) They keep a record and protect the patron in case his tickets are lost or stolen. (3) They keep the box office up to date on the number of tickets sold for every night of the production. (4) They constitute your best possible mailing list because they comprise your active stockholders.

One of the best arguments for the season ticket is that with a little more effort or expense than is required to sell a single ticket the theatre

FIG. 5.

After a letter is sent, the proof shown is supplied; it is then approved and returned.

The season audit stub is taken off when the season ticket is sold. It is a complete record of seat location, date and the name and address of your patron.

Audit stubs and tickets are all perforated so that they can be separated easily.

After season ticket sale is over, the remaining unsold tickets are broken down and sold for the single price shown for the single play. At this time the single audit stubs are retained as a check against sales which may be made daily.

can sell a package of tickets. Another argument is that a strong season sale insures a more balanced attendance—an unpopular show will have good-sized audiences as well as the popular one.

The season-ticket campaign with such advertising slogans as, "You get the best seats at the lowest prices," should account for 50 per cent or more of the ticket receipts for the year. These sales furnish a backlog of security to the theatre.

After the season ticket sale is over, usually after the first production, all unsold tickets should be disassembled and placed in the racks for single sales. It will not be necessary to stamp or mark any of them. If a ticket is not stamped "SEASON," the single price listed is automatic. The ticket sales can now be double checked by the small single audit stub on the left end of each ticket, which will be removed when the ticket is sold.

2. *Season tickets on coupon exchange.* Some theatres sell season tickets by issuing coupon books at a special discount. The coupons may be exchanged just before a production for any night of the run. The patron may apply all his coupons on any one of the performances, distribute them for all the shows, or use them in any combination he desires. Such an arrangement gives excellent flexibility for the customer and permits him to come at his convenience, but it has the disadvantage of drawing a small house on some nights and a large one on others. If a theatre is to succeed attendance must be stabilized as much as possible for every night of the production. It is a well-known fact that a Broadway theatre cannot survive unless there is a high average attendance; a full house now and then is not enough.

3. *Nonreserved season tickets.* Some theatres prefer not to reserve seats for their customers, but they do sell a packet of tickets at a reduced price with no seating preference—first come, first served. Such a system has definite advantages: seating is easier, people come earlier, and the problems of ushers and box office are almost nonexistent.

Organizations such as Civic Music and Community Concerts sell membership cards in advance. The events and the dates are listed on the card. Usually the card is punched when it is used and the patron surrenders it at the last event of the year. The membership drive is made before the cards are sold. There is no other sale of tickets or memberships after the one campaign. The members must have confidence that the officers of the organization will procure a satisfactory program for them. If they have a serious complaint, they can express it by dropping out the following year. This system has its disadvantages, but the fact that it has survived in so many communities is evidence of its merit.

4. *The standard reserved seat ticket.* This ticket, designed for the sale of a single performance without regard to any others, is probably more widely used than any other type. New York theatres and opera houses use it, as do theatres in most other American cities. Its popularity with big shows indicates that people are willing to pay a premium for the security of knowing where they will sit. If they wish to pay a top price, they can get a choice seat. The reserved ticket has come to mean that the show has a certain elegance and class. When people read that the seats are not reserved, they often suspect that the show is not of the highest quality.

A few theatres use a simple audit stub which is a half-inch perforated extension on the end of the ticket.

Sale Audit
Friday ev. May **8**
$1.50
Fed. tax exempt

If there are several different ticket sellers, the audit stubs make it possible to check each seller separately and thus to determine if any ticket seller is "long or short." Another value of the audit stub is that the box office always knows exactly how many tickets are left on the rack by simply subtracting the number of audit stubs from the house capacity. In most professional theatres there is no way of checking cash against sales until the "dead wood" (unsold tickets) are counted and the show is checked out completely. Training ticket sellers to tear off the audit stub when a sale is completed is a little annoying, but it is not difficult and the operation soon becomes a habit.

Whereas the cost of printing one set of tickets for one night can be prohibitively high, ordering tickets for a group of plays makes each set less expensive. Often it is an economy to purchase a year's supply even when the names and dates of the shows are not known. Such information

FIG. 6. These are samples of types of tickets to suit different needs.

1. Stanford University uses the pad-type season ticket for five plays. 2. Reserved-seat ticket with single audit stub. 3. A general admission ticket with the dignified appearance of a reserved seat ticket. 4. Variation on reserved-seat ticket without date specified. 5. Regular roll ticket.

can be imprinted by any job printer at a small cost. The major expense in a set of tickets is for printing seat numbers, rows, and sections. When this part of the cost is distributed over a dozen or more sets, the price of each is surprisingly reduced.

The use of the reserved seat ticket does increase operation costs—not only for the tickets themselves, but also for competent box-office staff, ushers, and extra services to patrons. On the other hand, a theatre of professional quality will find that the expense is justified: the management takes greater pride in the production, and the public feels that it has received a higher quality of entertainment. The use of this type of ticket may mean that little difference between the success and failure of your theatre.

5. *The unreserved-seat ticket.* This ticket is usually used in theatres in which row and seat numbers are not already affixed to the individual seats. Such tickets are consecutively numbered from one up through the quantity needed for each date or attraction. This unreserved-type of ticket, while not specifying a given seat, can specify a house part or section such as loge, main floor, or balcony. It can be placed on sale well in advance of the opening date and will also be of material help toward the success of any production. Some theatres have found it advisable to have the reserved-seat type of ticket printed for the main floor while the balcony is sold unreserved. This again depends upon the type of theatre, its location, the production, and the clientele to which it caters.

6. *The roll-type ticket.* Last but not least is the roll-type of ticket, which is used entirely for general admission. Since neither date or time is specified on this ticket, it is most often sold at the box office just prior to show time. Such tickets are sometimes carried as a stock item by the theatre management, they can be purchased inexpensively from any ticket printer. While general-admission roll-tickets are not considered advisable for the average production, they do, however, have a definite place for some attractions, such as children's matinees or movies.

What to Have Printed on the Tickets

It is surprising to note that from ten to fifteen items are printed on a reserved seat ticket, including name of the theatre; name of sponsor or producing organization; year, day of month, day of week, and hour of starting time, show and location of the seat—the section, row, and seat number are printed on both ends of every ticket; established price, state tax, federal tax, and sometimes city tax. If a ticket is set up to be sold at either a season price or a single sale price then both prices must appear on the ticket.

What to Do With Colors and Prices

After the proper type of ticket has been chosen and the admission prices decided upon, the colors should be selected. To avoid confusion it is well to use contrasting colors. Different colors in a set of tickets should mean different prices. When the color changes the price should change: if there are four different prices there should be four different colors.

It is often helpful to designate a particular color for a certain price throughout the house and to keep that combination throughout the year— or for a number of years, unless there is some good reason to change. To illustrate, a white ticket could mean the top price of $2.50; green might mean the second price, $2.00; pink could mean the third price, $1.50; and yellow the lowest price of $1.00. If a matinee or other performance were scaled fifty cents lower over the entire house, the top price and the white ticket would not be used. Much confusion and many questions can be eliminated by staying with a uniform application of color to price. Distinctive colors for each price will not only facilitate the handling of tickets at the box office by making different admission prices readily distinguishable, but the colors referring to different parts of the house will facilitate the seating of patrons when the rush comes.

V

THE BOX OFFICE: CENTRAL NERVE OF THE THEATRE

Of all places to attempt to save money, the box office should be positively the last. A good box-office employee will earn several times his salary; a poor one is a liability multiplied by the number of hours he works. It is true that the right kind of help is not easy to find and it will cost money, but if you cannot afford the best help you cannot afford a theatre.

Box-Office Personnel

Qualifications for box-office personnel should include ability to meet the public, a pleasant but businesslike attitude, accuracy, and honesty. Because the customer's only direct contact with the theatre personnel may be the ticket office, his impressions from that brief visit are most important.

If he is properly impressed by the courtesy and efficiency with which he is served he will be an agent of good will. On the other hand, if the customer feels that the attendant has no interest in the sale, he becomes suspicious about his purchase. At best the ticket buyer feels rather helpless because he seldom knows precisely what he has bought. A ticket is not a tangible piece of merchandise like a hammer or a pair of shoes. It is merely a contract printed on a small cardboard, the final value of which is in doubt until the show is over. Because the customer buys largely "sight unseen," he must have confidence in the box-office personnel.

Many people feel that the ticket seller will stoop to anything to get the customer's money and send him away. Even though the customer may have been sold choice seats, he often leaves with the haunting suspicion that he has been gyped. (The Romans had a word for it: *caveat emptor*—let the buyer beware.)

Box-Office Location

Believe it or not, a recent survey of Broadway theatregoers showed that one of the two leading reasons why patrons did not attend the theatre more often was "inaccessibility of tickets." This single deterrent accounted for 28.6 per cent of the stay-aways, and was the most amazing fact of the entire survey.

How could it be that more than a fourth of the prospective audience had been led to believe that "all tickets for all shows were virtually impossible to get"? Managers could understand the other reason for infrequent attendance, high prices, which accounted for 36 per cent of their trouble; but to have such ruinous misinformation broadcast about the ticket office was unthinkable.

Broadway does not have a monopoly on box-office problems. Hundreds of theatres, educational and others, are located where they are hard to find. If every theatre had a conveniently located ticket office where everyone could get honest, firsthand information, what a boon it would be! It is true that avid theatregoers and old standbys will find the box office no matter where you put it, but there are countless potential customers who might be induced to buy tickets if the questions of where, when, and how were given clear and simple answers.

It is an excellent idea to have a downtown box office in addition to one at the theatre. In every community there is some enterprising merchant willing to furnish advertising space, office space, telephone service, and sometimes box office assistance if need be. The first thing to look for is the best location. Choose a firm of dignity and prestige that can furnish sufficient space. It should be located on a main street. Book stores and music stores are often equipped to extend such assistance. The theatre can reciprocate by giving the name of the firm in connection with all its advertising about the box office. For example, newspaper, radio and television advertisements will say, "Tickets are on sale at Civic Pride Book Store, 150 Main Street." This is publicity that a store cannot buy.

Box-Office Hours

A word should be said about the hours for a box office. If theatre tickets are sold in a downtown store the hours should correspond to hours of the store. No matter where the box office is located, the advertised hours should be kept without fail. If the box office is advertised to open at 10 o'clock, the ticket seller should not be just arriving at ten; he should be ready for business. Box-office hours should be planned for convenience of the customers. The hours from 9 A.M to 6 P.M. are suggested, but local needs may determine a better schedule. By all means keep the office open during the noon hour. On days of the show the box office should be open from 9 A.M. to curtain time. If customers come and find no service because the box office is closed, they may not come back. Post a schedule of hours and stick to it. A theatre can get an amateurish reputation from don't-give-a-care box-office attendants just as easily as it can from its stage performances.

Box-Office Advertising

Failure to utilize your box office possibilities for advertising is a mistake. People who care enough about your show to buy tickets will often help you advertise if the idea is presented with dignity. How? (1) The box office should be properly decorated with pictures from the production. (2) Post all information about dates, starting time, and prices. (3) Include a map showing location of the theatre. (4) A seating plan should be available. (5) A small envelope for the tickets may carry an advertising slogan, such as "Seattle's Finest Entertainment" and have space to write the name and address of the purchaser. (6) A neat little advertising leaflet could be handy with the inscription, "Take one for a friend." The person who thought enough of your show to buy a ticket would recommend it to a friend.

It is dangerous advertising to have a ticket office resembling a glass cage with the ticket racks in full view of patrons. Prospective customers seeing the racks and not knowing the theatre seating plan or how the tickets are arranged may get a distorted idea of how many tickets are left and what they are. The deadly impression that the sale is bad can be picked up even though it is not true. Keep the tickets in a convenient rack or drawer away from the view of the public.

Box-Office Equipment

To function properly a box office must be fully equipped. First of all, reserved-seat tickets should be racked to suit the floor plan. All tickets must be within easy reach of the seller and arranged so as to show date, price, seat number, row, and section.

Necessary supplies include pencils, paper, staple machine, elastic bands, will-call file, regular envelopes, small ticket envelopes, postage stamps, money wrappers, paper clips, and a ticket punch. Other important equipment might include an adding machine, ticket-office chairs, fan or ventilator, a desk or table for counting money, a cabinet for supplies, and a safe.

A cash register or a cash drawer is most important for the efficient and accurate handling of money. A well-designed cash drawer which has a space for the different denominations of bills and coins is indispensable. If two or more persons are in the box office, each should have his own cash drawer.

A telephone is an essential part of box-office equipment. Its principal uses are to give information concerning tickets, prices and available seating, and to answer questions concerning the productions.

It is unfortunate that the word "box" was ever tacked on to "ticket office." To architects the word seems to have suggested a room barely large enough for one person to stand or sit. If you ever have an opportunity to specify dimensions of your box office, don't make the mistake of having it too small to serve its purpose. It should be a well-ventilated room, at least 6' × 10', with two windows plus an adjoining room where preparations, auditing, and counting of money can be done in privacy.

Box-Office Policies

The manager should see that there are definite policies with regard to the following:

1. Passes. A pass list has a way of growing like a cancer. Many an artist and many a theatre have been ruined by it. "Once a deadhead always a deadhead," is a truism of long standing. As surely as you give a person a free ticket, he will be back for another one next time. It's human nature. It is a sad fact that many people who receive passes can well afford to buy their tickets. There is, of course, no denying that a discriminate issuing of "Annie Oakleys" has great advantages. For example, newspaper, radio, and television personnel who work directly with theatre publicity must not be overlooked. Their support, or lack of it, can make or break your project. No one who deserves a pass should be left out. The manager should plan his pass list carefully, considering suggestions from the staff.

As far as possible, passes should be given only on the first night. But it invariably happens that some VIP expects a pass on the biggest night —hence the greeting, "You're as welcome as a pass at a sellout."

Some managers who became tired of being solicited for passes once prepared the following which expresses a common feeling about this most annoying problem:

Free Passes

IN THOSE DAYS THERE WERE NO PASSES GIVEN

"Search the Scriptures"

Thou shalt not pass. (Num. 20:18)
Though they roar, yet they cannot pass. (Jer. 5:22)
Suffer not a man to pass. (Judg. 3:28)
The wicked shall no more pass. (Nah. 1:15)
None shalt pass. (Isa. 34:10)
This generation shall not pass. (Mark 13:30)
Beware that thou pass not (II Kings 6:19)
There shall no strangers pass. (Amos 3:17)
Neither any son of man pass. (Jer. 2:43)
No man may pass through because of the beasts. (Ezek. 14:15)
SO HE PAID THE FARE THEREOF AND WENT. (Jonah 13)

---

2. *Refunds.* What does a ticket seller do when a customer returns, lays tickets down in front of him, and says: "I want a refund"? Which of the following offers the best solution?

(1) Make a refund graciously and without question so as to keep the customer's good will.

(2) Make a refund only if the customer becomes most insistent, gets angry, and makes a terrible scene.

(3) Make a refund only if the customer is reasonable and decent.

(4) Make no refunds.

(5) Consider each request with regard to conditions and reasons given for requesting the refund.

(6) Try to make an exchange for another night if possible and avoid the refund.

(7) Tell him that all refunds must be approved by the manager who is out.

The word "refund" is certain to stimulate unpleasant sensations in the nervous system of any ticket seller. But since it must be dealt with, it is well to face it realistically and draw up a policy that makes sense. Here is a suggested formula developed from the crucible of experience:

(1) Make no refunds within twenty-four hours of the performance—no exceptions even if you have a sellout. Next time there may not be a sellout. This is not easy, but if you have made a rule it will have to stand. If patrons insist on a refund in violation of policy, you might suggest that they give the tickets to a friend.

(2) Make no refunds at any time on season tickets after the first production is finished. Such tickets were purchased at a discount price, and refunding on them will be difficult for the bookkeeper as well as the box office.

(3) Refunds on single ticket sales may be made prior to the twenty-four hour limit. Such refunds should be made graciously in order to keep the patron's good will. If he goes away feeling that he has had a hard time to get his money back, he will keep away from your box office thereafter. It is bad enough to part with the money; there is no use losing a customer as well.

A few closing words about refunds: Everyone who works in the box office should tell the same story. They should learn to tell it pleasantly, but in a tone that is final. Such information should also be written and posted. If there is any weakness or loophole the patron will see it, because he is looking for it. No one likes a ticket seller who refuses to give him a refund. In fact ticket sellers as a group are not likely to inspire trust and confidence. The most maligned group of employees in the world are the Broadway box-office "gentlemen." Many doubt that even their mothers love them.

3. *Ticket selling.* Many advance announcements made through direct mail or in newspapers carry a statement of selling policy something like this: "Mail orders now—best seats go first. Requests will be filled strictly in order received." To most people that sounds like a fair enough promise, and smart managements will do well to keep that promise. The theatre has a perfect right to hold out such tickets as are needed for passes and house tickets to be used in emergency calls, but all others

should be sold in the order received. Honesty should forbid that an order which comes late be given preference over an earlier one. Moreover, if such unfairness is practiced, it will be found out—to the detriment of the theatre. Even when the box office is strictly honest it is hard—yea, impossible—to convince some people that their orders were filled in proper turn as they were received. The same person who will plead with the box office to fill his order ahead of others would be the first one to tell others how he did it.

It is good salesmanship to encourage customers to take their tickets on the nights when sales are lightest, and good technique to push the highest priced tickets; but this should not be overdone. Some ticket sellers have made themselves disliked by high-pressure methods. For example, if a novice goes to the box office and says, "Two tickets for tonight," he will see two of the highest priced tickets in front of him before he can say another word. If the buyer then says, "Oh, I can't pay that much," the seller picks them up painfully and drops two of the next highest price before the naive buyer. If the buyer again insists the price is too high, the ticket seller may locate two others, which he deposits on the counter with an air of exasperation which seems to say, "Take these and go. I can't understand why people like you are alive at all."

Hundreds of articles have been written about the rude deportment of box-office personnel, pointing out that lack of courtesy at the box office is a handicap of no little importance. On the other hand, the problem of selling tickets to the public can be extremely trying. People who would not question spending freely for a new car or a suit of clothes will argue about a seat location as if their lives depended on it.

Thomas J. R. Brotherton, a Broadway ticket seller, in his ironic article, "How to Run a Box Office," gives eleven pointers for the ticket seller to consider:

(1) You must be a mind reader.
(2) You must be polite but not familiar.
(3) Give people the seats they want, even if you have to get them back from the persons who bought them a week in advance.
(4) Never ask, "How many? What price? For when?" You are supposed to know that.
(5) Always wear a smile, even when being called a liar, and beg pardon for not knowing it without being told.
(6) When a lady stands for an hour or two selecting a seat, don't ask her why she didn't bring her sewing. She might do it next time.

(7) When a man comes up to the window smoking a bad cigar and blows smoke in your face, smile as if you like it, and ask him the brand. That will make him feel good.

(8) When a person leaves 25¢ of his change, be sure to call him back. Otherwise he will come back later and declare he left a dollar.

(9) When asked if the play is good, be sure to say "yes." You might as well; they won't believe you anyway.

(10) Study all periodicals, almanacs, timetables, weather reports, and so forth, as you never know what questions you may have to answer.

(11) When a lady asks for a balcony seat downstairs, don't look foolish. Give her a seat in the middle of the longest row so that she can't get out to give you hell.

4. Dressing the house. By a judicious distribution of tickets in the theatre, it is possible to make a small audience have the appearance of a reasonably large one. Such an impression makes both audience and actors feel better. In theatre parlance this technique is called "dressing the house." It means that the vacant seats should be scattered rather than leaving a block of empties in one place. Care should also be taken not to have the seating lopsided. It is almost unbelievable how the illusion of a large audience can be created by planned distribution.

If it is certain that a performance is not going to sell well, the proper way to dress the house is to remove from the rack a number of tickets from various parts of the house and sell all those remaining. This method will avoid confusion for the seller and needless discussion with the customers.

5. The telephone. Some theatres positively will not accept orders for tickets over the telephone. A few do not even have a telephone listing. This is especially true of professional houses in New York, Chicago, San Francisco, and other large cities. Such theatres have ticket brokers who may accept orders from persons they know. At the other extreme are the university and community theatres, which overuse the telephone and advertise the number to call for the box office.

Somewhere between the two extremes, the successful theatre should probably establish a policy that would serve the public without too much work and confusion at the box office. No theatre can afford to ignore telephone callers; moreover, public relations would require more intimate consideration for the people who are tax payers and public officials. The following suggestions gathered from experience of the theatre managers should be helpful:

(1) The telephone which is used for advertising purposes should not be the same as the box office telephone.

(2) Every call should be handled by an expert, because a good prospect is on the line and the wrong answers could lose him.

(3) If it seems absolutely necessary to take a reservation on the telephone, do it graciously. However, the prospect should be urged to send or bring in his remittance for tickets as soon as possible. The great trouble with the telephone order is that there is absolutely no way by which one can get money through it. Many people will have honest intentions, but still fail to pick up the tickets.

4) The box office should inform the prospective patron that it will be pleased to hold the tickets until a certain date. If the date goes by and the tickets are still not called for, urge him pleasantly to come for his tickets.

Every effort should be made to keep both the customer and his good will. He is a walking advertiser and you have no way of knowing where he will go or whom he will meet.

6. *Policy Conclusions.* Whatever the policy of the box office on any item, the management should make it as definite and as clear as possible. The decision should not be kicked around or changed to suit the convenience of some employee or patron. All customers should receive a written statement of box office policy with their purchase of tickets. In every theatre there are certain recurrent questions which should be explained in order to protect both customers and box-office employees. To say that there will be no exceptions may be over-emphatic, but if allowances are to be made, the conditions for such should be understood.

Employees of the theatre must be honest and forthright. The public will not be fooled—not for long. A traveling show may come to town and get by with a few misrepresentations, but a permanent group must conduct its business affairs on a high level. Good public relations should be maintained every day of the year.

It is hard for people to understand that tickets are a peculiar kind of merchandise that cannot be restocked or put back on the shelves to be sold later. When the date of the entertainment is past, all the tickets left on the rack are absolutely worthless; there is no merchandise more perishable. Hence it is important that the box office should do everything in its power to assist management and promotion. The old idea that a box office is merely a dispenser of tickets does not hold. It should be an integral part of the whole operation.

Establishing the Prices or "Scaling the House"

The following figures show a typical distribution of seats and prices for a theatre with seating capacity of 2,001. Preparing such information is known as "scaling the house." This task of evaluation or scaling of seats is an important duty of the manager, which requires not only a knowledge of the theatre, but also a knowledge of the production and the audience. For example, the prices in sections must be equitable and appeal to the public. Obviously the job of scaling the house should not be done in a hurry; it should be considered carefully, part by part.

The total amount of money which could be realized if every seat were sold according to the scale is called the "house gross." In this case the house gross for the 2,001 seats is $3,633. When the final box-office report is made, it will show what part of the capacity or house gross was actually sold in each price group. See example top of page 50.

Box-Office Reports

A well-prepared box-office report summarizes and condenses a great deal of information which will be a financial record as well as a valuable guide for the future. The report should be carefully prepared and include sufficient detail to give an accurate picture of financial status.

Ordinarily there are four kinds of box-office reports: (1) the daily report, (2) report of each performance, (3) report of the production, which may include several performances, and (4) the season report of all productions.

The daily report is a record of the number of tickets sold on a single day at each price. It gives a complete breakdown of cash on hand and the totals. The items included on a daily report may vary with the theatre; some will report student coupons, passes, unsold tickets, taxes, and net receipts as well as other information. A sample of a daily report is shown on page 52.

The report of each performance should include the total number of seats sold, the number unsold, various parts of the house and prices assigned to them, net receipts, taxes, and totals. This report should also

LOCATION	ESTABLISHED PRICE	NUMBER OF SEATS	GROSS MONEY
Main Floor			
Center			
Sec. B-C, Rows 1–15	$2.50	338	$ 845.00
Sec. B-C, Rows 16–27	$2.00	288	$ 576.00
Sides			
Sec. A-D, Rows 1–20	$2.00	342	$ 684.00
Sec. A-D, Rows 21–27	$1.50	148	$ 222.00
Lodge			
Center			
Sec. BCD	$2.50	129	$ 322.50
Sides			
Sec. A-E	$1.50	30	$ 45.00
Balcony			
Center			
Sec. BCD, Rows 1–4	$2.00	125	$ 250.00
Sec. BCD, Rows 6–10	$1.50	175	$ 262.50
Sec. BCD, Rows 11–18	$1.00	234	$ 234.00
Sides			
Sec. A-E, Rows 1–12	$1.00	192	$ 192.00
Total money without tax			$3,633.00

include the month, day, and year, the name of the show, and the name of the theatre. At the top of the report there should be an entry about the weather. Almost everywhere the weather is an important factor in show business. Extremes of weather should be described sufficiently to have meaning. A sample of this report is shown on page 53.

The production report compiles and summarizes the reports of individual performances. Full details need not be given: such items as the number of seats in each price bracket, color of tickets, and number of tickets unsold may be omitted. The total number of tickets sold and the total cash may be sufficient for this report.

The season report will compile financial information on all productions. These comprise the material for a study which may be highly rewarding for the officers of the theatre. The reports should be studied with care, for there is danger of jumping to conclusions. For example, a poor record for show number five might be the fault, not of the show itself, but of show number four which preceded it. Show number four was a "turkey" and had a damaging effect on those that followed. Along with the season reports, the box office should supply any information which may have been unusual such as date conflicts or catastrophes.

There may not be much romance or love at the box office, but it would be difficult to overstate its importance as the central nerve of the theatre. The manager, director, actors, and even the public are deeply concerned about the operations of this important spot. If the newspapers report to their thousands of readers that business is booming at the box office, everyone is anxious to join the rush; if it is reported to be dull or slow, people will stay away.

Theatres are always anxious to have stories and pictures of lively activity at the box office because that is the one place where action means continued business. Reputable theatre operators are idealists, and they sense that they have a responsibility to the public to produce plays that are worthwhile; but they are also realists, and they know all too well that unless the box office is consistently active it will soon be curtains.

NOTE: The following report (Fig. 8) represents a near capacity sale with excellent weather conditions. Theatres generally do not count on more than 65% of capacity. That the tickets on this show were equitably priced is shown by the even distribution of sale. There were 55 passes, which is probably too many. This box office form is simple and easy to reproduce. Any other necessary details can be inserted. Use of the arabic numbers on the left is optional, but they enable one to check and audit more easily.

DAILY BOX OFFICE REPORT

Production: *Arms and the Man*

Date: April 20, 1970

Currency:

Twenties	......	$100.00
Tens	......	40.00
Fives	......	55.00
Ones	......	23.00

TOTAL: $218.00

Silver:

Dollars	......	$ 27.00
Halves	......	16.00
Quarters	......	14.00
Dimes	......	.40
Nickles	......	.10

TOTAL: $ 57.50

Checks:

TOTAL: $ 14.00

GRAND TOTAL: $289.50

Audit Stub or Ticket Count:

54	@	$2.00	$108.00
121	@	1.50	181.50

TOTAL: $289.50

_____
Signature

Over or Under $ 00.00

FIG. 7.

BOX OFFICE REPORT

Civic Theatre
(capacity 2001)

Production: _Othello_

Date: March 20, 1970
Weather: Excellent

House Part	Ticket Color	Capacity	Sold	Unsold	Price Each	Totals
Main Floor:						
1. Rows 1-20 (B-C center)	white	458	403	55	$3.00	$1209.00
2. Rows 21-27 (B-C center)	pink	168	168	0	2.00	336.00
3. Rows 1-9 (A & D sides)	blue	110	110	0	3.00	330.00
4. Rows 11-27 (A & D sides)	yellow	380	360	20	2.00	720.00
Loges:						
5. Rows 1-3 (BCD center)	red	129	129	0	3.00	387.00
6. Side loges (A & E)	green	30	20	10	2.00	40.00
Balcony:						
7. Rows 1-10 (BCD center)	coral	300	300	0	2.00	600.00
8. All other balcony	gray	426	401	25	1.00	401.00
Total Seats 2001				**GRAND TOTAL**		$4023.00
Passes 55						

FIG. 8.

VI

SELLING THE SHOW

More theatres are on their way to extinction because of amateurish management, poor publicity and bad public relations than for any other reason. The sad part of it is that they refuse to face up to their problems; it is easier to rationalize and die valiantly.

The Promotion Man and His Job

On this subject of management and promotion, a highly successful manager, Richard Hoover, of the Pittsburgh Playhouse, in a special letter to the American National Theatre and Academy gives advice which could serve as a blood transfusion to many groups:

I sincerely believe that a full-time employee to coordinate the activities of your group and to serve as financial administrator would undoubtedly be helpful. We have observed so many operations where a high degree of professionalism has been attained in the production field while the rankest sort of amateurism prevailed in the administrative department. For some inexplicable reason, men who in their own business are realistic and efficient, permit artistic enterprises which they serve as board members to flounder through incompetent business management.

I should like to point out to you the two courses your theatre can follow in selecting a business manager—and some of the problems of each course.

First, you may employ a secretary-bookkeeper whose principal function is to maintain records and to relieve volunteer committee chairmen of routine duties. This individual need not be a theatre person—in fact probably should not be—as the function of the job would be that of an executive secretary of any civic or service organization.

On the other hand, you might elect to employ a theatre business manager whose functions would include promotion as well as those of an executive secretary.

Mr. Hoover's suggestions will be echoed by other able managers. It is certainly true that the promotion and management division is the weakest link in many theatres. In almost every other profession or trade the rule is to call in an expert when something is wrong. Even the theatre director must have been trained and have had considerable experience before he can be fully accepted. But it is generally assumed that almost anybody can promote or manage. The job is looked upon as being the most artless, unimaginative of all theatre work.

How are managers and publicity men or women chosen? The two most common methods are both hopeless:

1. Ask someone to take over the publicity who really wanted to act in a play, but was rejected as not good enough. Explain to him that he is a fine fellow whom the theatre needs. Some day (if the theatre gets really hard up) there may be a part for him. Right now, however, the exigency is for a publicity man, one who can write up the stories and sell the show which he was not good enough to be in. Because the would-be actor loves the theatre he accepts the publicity assignment as a sort of consolation prize. Such a choice is a dreadful mistake for the theatre. A man who merely knows nothing about a job might learn; but a man who knows nothing about it and on top of that has no interest will contribute nothing.

2. The second method is almost as bad as the first. The theatre appoints a committee to the job. Under this arrangement each one often thinks that somebody else is doing it; or somebody fails to go ahead for fear of doing something wrong. It is quite possible that none of the members have any information about the problems. If a committee is to be effective it must have a strong chairman and cooperative members. Anyone who does not work should be replaced by someone who will. Of course the committee must work as a unit. If one member gives or changes an order, it should come through the chairman. Otherwise the person receiving directions will be confused. He may find himself in the same position as the Indian who was building a canoe, and getting along well until a white man came along and said, "Oh, don't do it that way, scoop it out here and here." Others came and gave him advice and finally when the canoe was finished and he pushed it into the water, it tipped over on its side. A typical committee production. So the disillusioned Indian pulled it onto the bank, cut himself another tree, and started all over. No sooner had he got things nicely under way than a white man arrived and said,

"Oh, don't do it that way, let me tell you how I would do it." The Indian who was now much wiser, pointed to the blunder and said, "There is everybody's canoe over there; you can work on that. This one will be mine."

The ideal publicity man is easy to describe but hard to find. He should be one who is businesslike and knows how to get things done. Because he is continually working with people who are under pressure, he must be tactful, cheerful, and encouraging. A high regard for other peoples' time is important. A newspaper editor can get very tired of a press representative who overstays his welcome. He should have a dignity and bearing which command respect. That he should have a thorough knowledge of the theatre program, its plays, problems, and objectives, goes without saying. If he is timid and thin-skinned he will be miserable; he must know how to take rebuffs, criticisms, and disappointments and come back with the resiliency of a rubber ball. A pleasant smile and a good sense of humor will help a great deal. Above all, he must have imagination, the ability to see new angles and new methods of approach. That is a big order to ask for any one man, but almost all of the requisites are necessary to successful operation.

The Importance of a Good Product

"We, the promoters of entertainment, hold this truth to be self-evident: That before you sell something you must have something to sell." This aphorism is so deceptively simple that it should be repeated often. Nothing, absolutely nothing, can compensate for a poor production. If the quality of the show is sacrificed to pay social debts or to satisfy any other pressures rather than to furnish entertainment, your theatre is facing the setting sun. The entertainment which you advertise must be one in which you have explicit confidence. When you sell the show there must not be a note of doubt in your voice or a flicker of uncertainty in your eye. You must be proud of the product. You must feel secure in your statements about the quality and value of your entertainment.

If, for instance, you announce that you have a comedy that will furnish two hours of delightful entertainment, you had better produce just that —don't let anyone tell you that your audience will be delighted to have you surprise them with an additional thirty to sixty minutes. Chances are ten to one that many of your audience are clocking you; others measure

time accurately by the way they feel inside—some people are so gas-
tronomically timed that even ten extra minutes will cause them physical
pain. When there is so little to gain and so much to lose by running over-
time, this fault should be corrected; yet few producers heed the audiences' complaint, "The show was too long." When Paul Gregory and
Charles Laughton were staging their production *John Brown's Body*,
starring Raymond Massey, Judith Anderson, and Tyrone Power, they
decided that the show was running fifteen minutes too long for the comfort of the audience. Accordingly, they cut the production so that it
played within two hours including the intermission. Mr. Gregory, in com-
menting on the decision to cut, said, "If you keep an audience for more
than two hours, you are leading with your neck." When moderate length
of a show with top-flight artists is regarded as so important by profes-
sionals, is it not even more important for the less experienced to be
cautious about the overlong play?

There are amateur promoters who imagine that because they are dealing with intangibles they may be allowed to make certain misrepresentations in advertising. Such illogical thinking can lead to the loss of a good
name. The reputations of the theatre, the producer, the director, the
manager, even the complete organization, can be lost almost overnight.
What has taken years to build can dwindle quickly to the point where it
cannot be rebuilt. Shakespeare has Iago say,

> Good name in man or woman, dear my lord,
> Is the immediate jewel of their souls.

According to the Food, Drug, and Cosmetic Act of 1939, those who
compound prescriptions or manufacture and package food must label
and describe the contents and show the exact weight of their packages.
If they give wrong or misleading information and get caught in their
misrepresentations (and thousands have been) they can be fined or sent
to jail. The law carries an additional promise that if such violators make
use of the government mails to distribute any improperly labeled packages or ship them across state lines they may be sent to a federal prison.
Violations of the Food and Drug Act are more easily proved than is fraud
in entertainment, because tangible products can be examined, analyzed,
weighed, and tested in a laboratory. In show business, misrepresentations
are harder to nail down. "How does one prove that my so-called enter-

tainment is not really entertaining?" says the "turkey" producer. Ah! But people will know that you cheated them even if they cannot show the labeled package as evidence. We should take a lesson from the Food, Drug, and Cosmetic Act and tell people honestly what we have in the bottle. It might even be advisable to tell them occasionally what is not in it, as druggists sometimes do to allay doubts. For example, "This bottle is pure entertainment, and it contains no propaganda or sleep-inducing drugs. It will not cause hives or shingles." "But," recalls the sharp pro-moter, "Barnum said, 'There is a sucker born every minute!'" That may be true, but the chances are small for your collecting an entire audience of them at one time. The theatre man queries: "Who will apprehend me if I misrepresent the show? Who can point me out?" The answer is this: "Mr. John Q. Public will eventually take care of you." He is not only your victim, but simultaneously your policemen, jury, prosecuting attorney, and judge. Your punishment may not be swift, but it will be certain. When you are found guilty, you may be given the terrible "let alone" treatment; you may be banished, exiled, or starved. Thousands have been. Once the public turns against you it is slow to forgive, slower to forget. You may present ten excellent shows and one "turkey," and the public mind will dwell upon that "turkey" to the exclusion of all that was good. Some people, like old-timers, love to linger over a fiasco and recount its details as if it had been the Johnstown flood or the San Francisco earthquake. An old English rhyme laments:

> When I did well, I heard it never;
> When I did ill, I heard it ever.

In summary, tell your patrons what you will give them, "scout's honor," and do nothing less than your level best to deliver it. Finally, be certain that it is priced right. Don't forget the great man who said with tears in his eyes, "Honesty is the best policy; I have tried both."

Appeals to Buy Entertainment

When people buy entertainment or anything else for that matter, it is because of the pressure of certain motives which may or may not be reasonable or logical. Psychologists have given these motives such names as impulses, inducements, urges, and drives. For the purpose of this discussion, let us call them impelling motives.

THERE ARE TWO SETS OF ARGUMENTS ABOUT THEATRE GOING

FOR		AGAINST

It's the best anti-worry tonic.
  It makes me ten years younger.
It keeps me sane.
  We need to get out.
	Self
	Preser-
	vation
		I'm too tired.
		  Weather is bad.
		It kills me to sit so long.
		  We need to rest.

Best entertainment for the
  money spent.
A price for every purse.
  An investment, not a luxury.
	Property	We can't afford such prices.
		  It's cheaper to watch T-V.
		We get the worst seats
		  every time we go.

It adds to my prestige.
  Keeps me up to date.
It feeds my starved ego.
  We meet nice people.
It relaxes me.
	Power	It's all Greek to me.
		  It's too hard to park.
		They ignore us patrons.
		  They're a bunch of snobs.
		It wears me out.

It's sexy.
  I love a heart-warming story.
My family loves to go.
  I meet all my friends there.
	Affec-
	tions
		It's not sexy.
		  What do I care about
		frustrated people.
		  My wife is not interested.
		It corrupts our kids.

They say the show is good.
  It's a good place to be seen.
The theatre has status here.
  I want to see what critics
are talking about.
  The author is famous.
Let's keep up with the Joneses.
	Reputa-
	tion
		They say the show is lousy
		The critics panned it.
		  It's long hair and stuffy.
		Never heard of the author.
		  Shakespeare? He's dead.
		They say it didn't let out
		  till midnight.

I like to dress up and go.
  The show is delightful.
I like thrills and chills.
  What an attractive theatre–
It's different and it's fun.
	Tastes	I hate to dress up.
		  It's dull, trite stuff.
		I want entertainment,
		  not depressive problems.
		What an ugly old place–

The community needs
  the theatre.
It's our duty to support it.
  We've got to help out.
	Duty	It's not my headache.
		  Those who want it can
		worry about it—not me.
		  The theatre be damned!
		What good is it?

If first we divide them into seven categories we can get a better general working knowledge of these motives. In the next step we can indicate how they may be applied specifically to selling the show.

1. *Self preservation* means the desire for life and health. We seek freedom from worry and fear.

2. *Property* includes the appeals for financial gain. It covers money, bargains, profits, and financial deals.

3. *Power* is the desire to possess skill, leadership, and prestige. It includes control over others.

4. *Affections* may refer to anything including sex and love. A motive which touches our loved ones—brothers, sisters, sweethearts, wives, or children, gets action.

5. *Reputation* includes the desire for the good opinion and good will of others. The value of a good name is universally recognized.

6. *Duty* refers to our feelings of fairness, honesty, justice, patriotism, and common decency.

7. *Tastes* refers to aesthetic pleasure. We go to the theatre for enjoyment and pure entertainment. It is and should be the most common reason for buying a ticket to a show.

Armed with the confidence that you have a worthwhile product, you then must plan a systematic campaign to build an audience. Just telling the people what your product is and where they can find it will seldom suffice. The promoter's business is to get an audience into the theatre, not merely to pass out the information. You have a rack of tickets to sell. How can you do it? What media are open to you? How can you get the people to buy these tickets and come to your entertainment? There are many ways, some of which are obvious and well-known. But a few are obscure and hard to find. All of them require hard work. Let us evaluate a few of the most perfected and productive methods for selling the show.

VII

DIRECT MAIL HITS THE BULL'S-EYE

When a hunter wants a deer or an elk, he takes a rifle for a direct hit. When he hunts pheasants, ducks, or squirrels, he uses a shotgun. In show business, direct mail may be compared to the hunter with a rifle, in that he aims directly at a specific, prize target.

Direct mail will often find a valued customer whom you cannot reach by any other medium or method. Whereas the results of most advertising are so intangible that they cannot be assayed, the effectiveness of direct mail can be tabulated with considerable accuracy. Best of all, your direct mail offers the most in return for the least money. Well-established theatres and music groups sell more than 85 per cent of all their tickets by direct first-class mail; only 15 per cent are sold by all other media combined.

Build a Mailing List With Care

For this important medium, your theatre will save both time and money by setting up a suitable system for listing the names, addresses and telephone numbers of all prospective customers. Of the various filing systems, the one most commonly used is the inexpensive and flexible 3" × 5" card. On each card the surname or last name should appear first. The listing of each name, address, and telephone number must be absolutely accurate before it is filed alphabetically. If this simple system is properly set up, names may be added, changed, or removed without disturbing the list. Furthermore, these small cards are most convenient when addressing mail, in that several people can divide the mailing-list cards and work simultaneously without causing the slightest disorder or confusion. The customer's name should be placed at the top of the card rather than in the center, so that it can easily be seen and also because this leaves room for information about the customer. Such data as the fact that he bought six tickets in a given year can be quickly completed with a small date stamp. If the individual is a "patron" or "booster," such information can be kept on the file card. When mail is addressed, care should be taken to see that names are copied on the envelopes correctly. If the envelope has a misspelled name or wrong initial that is the first thing your prospective customer will notice, and he won't like it. If the addresser is in a hurry and writes down an inaccurate address, the letter will be lost. The post office reports that tremendous quantities of mail are lost because of careless or improper addressing.

Another suggestion on the mechanics of listing has to do with repeating the same name in the card file. If the filing clerk is not alert it is possible to have duplicate, triplicate, or even quadruplicate entries. For instance, a check of one file revealed four entries for the same person at the same address: Henry R. Pearson, H. R. Pearson, Henry Pierson, and Mary Pearson, his wife. Before you enter a new name, make sure it is really new and that you do not already have it listed in another form.

In addressing envelopes it is well worth the extra trouble to direct the mail to Mr. and Mrs. John Doe at their home address rather than to John Doe at his office.

(*Preferred addressing*)	(*Less effective*)
(Return) Dr. and Mrs. Frank Whiting 2036 Seabury S. W. Minneapolis, Minnesota	(Return) Dr. Frank Whiting University of Minnesota Minneapolis, Minnesota

Busy men, and some not so busy, have been known to forget to tell their dear wives about such matters; and, since your letter concerns the man and his wife, you may as well send it to both in the first place. It is well known, though not generally acknowledged, that some wives make all decisions in matters of selecting entertainment; if those wives do not receive the information firsthand it is a loss to the theatre.

The actual building of a mailing list requires that you make use of every possible technique to find the names of potential customers. To the enterprising and resourceful promoter the initial problem of getting a list, although difficult, is by no means impossible. A good mailing file is not easy to come by nor is it cheap. It requires the searching attention of an expert or several experts, both to build it and to maintain it properly. The money spent on building a really active list is the best investment in the whole advertising program. Someone who really cares should be in charge of this important work. If one is starting from scratch, any or all of the following methods will be effective:

1. Find the key people who are actively interested in dramatic entertainment and get them to suggest names of prospective customers.

2. Circulate a number of 3×5-inch cards at the theatre, on which your patrons may supply names and addresses of persons who may wish to be on your mailing list. Be sure to double check such information whenever possible.

3. Record the names received from newspaper responses. At the bottom of your newspaper advertisement, place a "mail-order coupon." Make the coupon large enough to get all the information needed—name, address, and telephone number.

4. Obtain a prospect list through a reputable stenographic or mailing service. There may be such a service in your city which would address a list for a fee of about $10 a thousand, or you may often buy such a list outright for $15 to $30 a thousand, depending upon its quality and selectivity. This purchase price of a list of names would not ordinarily include addressing; you would have to pay extra for that. Such lists are compiled under a variety of classifications such as "home owners," "householders," "professional people," and "industries and firms." It may be that some stenographic service has a list selected to suit your needs. A telephone call to several stenographic services will help to answer your questions. The best lists may cost a little more, but they will be worth it.

5. It is an excellent idea to get in touch with families moving into the area. With everything strange to newcomers, they are more likely to welcome your suggestions on entertainment. If you wait until after they have established their habits of living and found for themselves their places of entertainment, it will not be so easy to attract them to your theatre. A note of welcome and an explanation of your program presented at the right time will do wonders.

How does one find out the names and addresses of these newcomers? There are several productive methods.

(a) Consult the local power and light or other utility company. In smaller cities lists of newcomers may be released by such firms.

(b.) The local chambers of commerce often have fresh lists available.

(c.) In a civic organization it is not hard to get capable help to cover this whole assignment handsomely. Volunteer representatives who are well informed and can make a good impression might visit new subdivisions to find friends for the theatre. The committee on new memberships can be divided into geographic areas so that the coverage will be complete.

d. Watch the newspapers. They collect a great deal of information on new residents and often feature those who are likely to be active, talented, and civic-minded.

This work is never completed, and it requires the attention of a tactful and pleasant person. In every city some old friends are moving out and new people are moving in. Obituaries give the sad news of many staunch supporters. A new generation which knows little about the theatre is growing up and will have to be sold on the whole idea. All these changes should be incorporated in the mailing list, along with changes of address. The manager should constantly be alert for new names. For example, when he finds an enthusiastic patron he should ask him to suggest additional friends. Bad impressions can be created by continued mailing of announcements to the address of a patron ten years deceased.

The mere size or bulk of the mailing list is no criterion of its value. It should contain only the names of active purchasers and good prospects. A more select list can be maintained by checking the mailing list annually against orders received and putting a number or other symbol on the file cards of responding names. Such a system will sift out the names which have discontinued interest in the theatre, although one must be cautious about throwing out names which only seem to be inactive. It is possible to throw away a pearl. If there is doubt about the value of a name, make sure that it should not be on your list before you drop it. A telephone call or post card will usually provide the answer.

The Post Office Will Check the Mailing List

The problem of ascertaining who is deceased and who has changed his address can be inexpensively solved by means of an occasional United States Post Office verification. For only five cents per card, the post office will check every name and address on your list and return it with corrections and comments on every card such as "O. K." "deceased," "moved," or other appropriate mark. This most valuable service is not generally known, though it could not be duplicated for several times what you would have to pay your post office. It is listed and described in *The Postal Manual* as follows:

For correction of mailing list a minimum of $1 payable by cash, money order, or postal note shall be made at all post offices for the correction of any mailing list bearing less than twenty names and *for any list of twenty names or more a charge of five cents for each name submitted likewise payable in advance* shall be made. Lists will be returned free of postage. Furthermore all lists submitted, whether for correction of address or elimination of duplicates, are to be considered mailing lists at first-, second-, third-, and fourth-class post offices.

Users of this postal service have found it to be complete and thorough. No system of checkup is more satisfactory, timesaving, and economical.

When your mailing list is correct and complete, it represents the most valuable medium known to theatre advertising. Because it is a special list tailored to your needs, you should guard its use. Under no circumstances should it be lent or rented, as this would tend to destroy its value to you. If there is such a thing as a trade secret, this is it.

Can We Afford to Use First-Class Mail?

Perhaps our question should be, "Can we afford *not* to use first-class mail?" Relatively unimportant reminders and bulletins may be sent by third class, but it is good business to send all important sales announcements first class. Don't let anyone talk you into sending them any other way. The evidence is all against it. If the campaign letter isn't worth first-class mailing, you may as well throw it in the wastebasket yourself. Any doctor, lawyer, or business executive will tell you that second- third- and fourth-class mail is often thrown away without even a glance: Many busy executives say to their secretaries, "Don't bother me with anything except first-class mail; throw the rest of it in the wastebasket." Post offices are so loaded down with second-class and third-class matter that the congestion has often caused serious problems in service. In Congress, senators and representatives have actually referred to it as "trash mail." During a recent investigation, a United States senator expressed a common opinion when he said, "Trash mail, most of which goes into the wastebasket unread, pays only a fraction of its cost."

When, by implication, you say to your customer, "I didn't think this information was worth sending first class, "he is very likely to say to himself, "I agree entirely with you." The price of preparing and addressing an attractive mailing piece ranges from eight to twelve cents. Why run the risk of losing it en route for the sake of one extra penny to give it a mark of honor? One or two additional ticket orders could pay the difference between the first and third-class postal service of your entire list.

Another important benefit of first-class mailing is that if a return address is included, all undelivered items are automatically returned to the sender, thus enabling him to correct the list promptly. Undelivered mail of second, third, and fourth class is returned to the sender only if it carries the notation, "Return Postage Guaranteed." When such mail is returned, the sender must, of course, remit the postage. If the items are scarcely worth their postage, the only reason for having them returned would be to correct the mailing list.

Often, when mailing rooms are crowded, everything except first-class mail is set aside. This loss of even a few days in the delivery of your mailing piece may greatly reduce or even destroy entirely its effectiveness.

As mentioned previously, certain types of mail do not need to go first class. To meet the great variety of needs, the post office classifies mail as follows:

First Class: includes letters; postal and post cards; all matter wholly or partly in writing, and letters sealed or closed against inspection.

Second Class: includes newspapers and periodicals put out by their publishers.

Third Class: includes merchandise, catalogues, circulars, and printed matter under 16 ounces.

Fourth Class: includes merchandise, catalogues, and printed matter weighing 16 ounces or over.

"Bulk mail" is a term used to describe third-class mail which is tied in bundles and sent under a permit. Use of such a permit requires that there must be a prepared statement for the post office which declares the number of pieces being sent. If you are mailing 2,000 or more pieces third class it will pay you to buy a post office permit (this costs $20 and allows unlimited use for the calendar year) which allows you the bulk rate of 2½ cents for each piece, or 16 cents a pound, whichever is greater; the rate without a permit would be a minimum of 3 cents for each piece. However, if you have fewer than 4,000 pieces of mail in a year it would obviously be cheaper to use the nonbulk rate of 3 cents a piece up to 2 ounces. The savings of ½ cent on the first 4,000 would be exactly $20, or the price of the bulk mail permit. All mail over the 4,000 pieces would show a saving.

If the mail is sent from a nonprofit organization such as an educational institution or civic or educational theatre, the minimum price is 1¼ cent for each piece weighing 1.28 ounces or less though the rate of 16 cents a pound remains the same. Approval for a "nonprofit" designation must be obtained from the post office when nonprofit specifications have been satisfactorily proved.

When bulk mail is sent, the pieces must be sorted into separate bundles for each city, tied, and labeled accordingly. If there are fewer than ten pieces going to several different cities in one state, the bundle should be labeled "All for Iowa," or "All for Colorado," etc. If all the mail is being sent to one city, there is, of course, no problem of sorting. If bulk mail is sent without stamps affixed, which it usually is, the proper indicia must be printed on the envelope in accordance with bulk-mailing regulations. This includes a Statement of Mailing privilege and the permit number. There is also an additional fee of $10. for such mailing service. This fee is paid only once (it is used at least once every twelve months), but the $20 permit is paid annually, on a calendar year basis.

Even with bulk mail, it is possible to get notice of changes of any address by printing the following message in the lower left-hand corner of the envelope: "Form 3547 requested." A specific request of Form 3547 will give one of two results:

1. If the addressee has moved but has guaranteed forwarding postage, and the new address is known to the post office, the letter will be forwarded. A report, Form 3547, giving the new address will be furnished to you, the sender, for a service charge of five cents.

2. If the addressee has moved and his new address is unknown to the post office, the letter will be returned to the sender for three cents, the regular charge for third-class mail. If the addressee has died, the letter will be returned marked "deceased." The post office does not attempt to give the new location of the departed.

A Word About Envelopes

The government stamped envelopes sold at any post office is a combination value of envelope and stamp that is hard to beat. Printers and paper supply houses will agree. An equally good bargain is the government price of $2 a thousand for imprinting the return name and address of the sender in the upper left-hand corner. However, it should be noted that the government printing job requires from four to five weeks and cannot be rushed. The mills of the government grind slowly, and few theatres plan ahead far enough to avail themselves of the bargain price offered by the post office. Another note regarding envelopes is that they are available only in white. Inasmuch as a colored envelope is often desirable and the time factor vital, the manager may not wish to consider the use of government envelopes.

A few comparisons of post office prices with those of commercial houses may be helpful in making decisions. The price of the large envelope (U.S. No. 8, 4⅛″ × 9½″) with a 4 cent stamp is $47.60 a thousand—envelopes $7.60 and stamps $40.00. An envelope of similar quality purchased from a printer will cost about $11 a thousand—shows an advantage of over $3 for the government envelope. Moreover, this eliminates the tedious job of affixing a thousand stamps, which is a consideration of importance. A small item with regard to a large mailing, is that a few of the attached stamps invariably fall off, whereas the government stamp is built in. Every secretary has frowned at the almost impudent annoyance of "Insufficient Postage" boldly stamped on returned mail. There is no use to silently malign the postal clerk who rejects your letter, for he cannot tell the difference in an envelope that has lost its postage and one that never had any.

What to Mail

People will inevitably prejudge your show by its advertising. When you spend money for publicity, it turns out somehow that the best is the least expensive. Above all things, the information you mail out should be clear in its layout and complete in its detail. Be sure that you answer the following questions in your mailed announcement—in all paid advertising for that matter:

1. *What* is being offered?
2. *When* will it be? The month? The day? The hour?

3. *Where* will it be given? Is the theatre location easy to reach, or do customers need directions to find it?

4. *Tickets?* The range of prices for which locations?

5. *Who* sponsors it?

Secondly, the brochure should be interesting and attractive. It should make your prospective buyer say, "This looks like something we must see." The whole appearance of the mailing piece should imply, "We are proud of this offering; it is our very best." But too often it seems to say, "This production hardly deserves your attention; besides, we're more interested in saving pennies than we are in the business of entertainment."

The kind of play—comedy, mystery, or tragedy—should suggest the proper type of art and descriptive material. Photographs, color, cartoons, and clever sketches are eye-catchers. Proper arrangement on the page will also enhance the advertisement. Size, shape, and balance are all prime considerations in designing an attractive mailing piece.

Just exactly how many pieces should your announcement envelope contain? One or two or three or four? Some publicity writers prefer to include the mail-order blank as a portion of the announcement sheet. Others enclose a special order blank plus a return envelope. Some even advocate a postage-paid envelope.

Every manager or director of publicity will, of course, make his own decisions. It is generally believed to be good sales psychology to make a job as easy and simple as possible for the customer. A potential buyer may not need much obstruction to stop him from sending in the order. If everything is ready and entirely convenient, he will send it in. Even so small a task as finding an envelope and addressing it, or finding a postage stamp, may lose an order.

We can summarize in this way: If what you are selling is something that your prospective customer wants, and wants very much, he will be certain to get his order in the mail in spite of any little inconveniences. But if, in the first place, he is only lukewarm about buying your product, any obstacle—however small—will stop him cold.

Once upon a depression time, about 1932, a western university with a large new auditorium, accepted the rare opportunity to book three performances of Earl Carroll's *Vanities*. From every angle it was a daring venture. Entertainment everywhere was on the rocks. But a more serious question than financial failure was the appropriateness of a state university in a conservative community importing such a sophisticated production. Eyebrows were arched when the first public announcement and the glamorously enticing pictures of some of the dancing girls appeared in papers and on bill boards. It was known that such risqué things went on in New York, but one never expected to find them in a western city where moral standards were high.

The purists and the "do-gooders" went to work to explain why people should not attend the show. The gossips soon picked up the refrain and word of mouth advertising was tremendous. It was also much exaggerated. Rumor was abroad that the show would demoralize the youth and corrupt the old. Some self-styled defenders of decency got on the telephone and cautioned people to keep away from this scantily clad revue. The box office could tell how fast such phone calls were going out by the rate of people coming in. When one eminent citizen who deplored the venture was asked if he had ever seen the show, he replied, "Yes, I saw it three times in New York, but I go to watch the staging and lighting effects." The *Vanities* became a civic issue. Consequently, people decided that they had better check it firsthand even though the tickets were expensive. Somehow people found the money for choice seats. The older men explained that they had to have the seats down close because their wives had bad ears, or bad eyes, or both. The young people and the naive bought all the cheaper seats with the net result that by the time the *Vanities* arrived, there was standing room only. Here was a city of high moral standards in the throes of a depression when nobody had any money and, presto, a sellout.

There was one more item of interest: After the show, and it turned out to be an exciting one, many people were certain there must have been something wrong or they would not have had so much fun. The president and the regents were so besieged with protests that they met and issued a proclamation that this kind of show should never again come to the fair campus, and the proclamation still stands.

The incident taught two valuable lessons in show business which should not be overlooked: (1) There are people who will look you straight in the eyes and tell you a lie. True, they will predict that your show will fail and then make it a success by giving it support. (2) If people really want something they will pay for it even though they can't afford it. And obversely, if they don't want it, they won't buy it no matter how good it is for them.

Because most sales are made on initial contacts, there should be considerable incentive to get immediate response. The longer a person postpones sending in his order, the less likely he is to send it at all. Hence, the mailed advertising should carry plenty of hurry-up come-ons such as:

"Best seats go first."

"Save 30 per cent and buy season."

"Don't be left out."

"Act now."

"For best service send your mail order today."

"All requests filled promptly in the order in which they are received."

"This discount ticket offer expires on _____."

"All seats reserved."

"Save money and time—order now!"

Because there is no way by which the public can be coerced to attend the theatre, the advertising must be persuasive and enticing. Military service and taxes are thrust upon us, but entertainment is something which people, especially Americans, can live without. Perhaps the best angle for selling the show is to feature it for what it is or ought to be— entertainment. Is it not a fair division of labor to let the churches do the preaching and Western Union deliver the messages, while the theatres furnish entertainment? There is no objection to a play that teaches, no objection to a play that has a great message or to one that brings forth any valuable by-product; but such extras should come as by-products without special effort or design. The chief business of the theatre has always been and still is entertainment, even though propagandists have sought to use it as a tool.

Those who have had experience with mail orders know the pattern of response: the big returns come during the first few days. If the mail reaches the prospective customers on Friday, the biggest response will come on the following Tuesday. It takes the weekend and Monday to clear the post office. There follow two or three large days, then a gradual falling off and a fadeout.

Mailing Brochures Must Be Well Planned

The guiding principle in the preparation should be that you are marketing entertainment to people who can take it or leave it. The following sample layouts have all been found effective in the areas in which they were used, but because they have worked in one community does not guarantee that they will work in every community. There are hundreds of types of brochures.

When to Mail It

Timing of the mailing is extremely important to its value. Ordinarily, managers and promoters recommend that advance notices go out a month to six weeks before the show. Announcements in the newspapers should follow about a week after the mailing. Regular patrons of your mailing list deserve the courtesy of an advance notice. If your regular customers understand that they have been given a little special attention and consideration they will have a better incentive to respond promptly. If your advertisement in the paper appears at the same time the mail goes out, the purpose of the direct mail is partly vitiated.

Other things being equal, it is advisable to have the mailing arrive at the homes just after pay day, which is usually around the first or the fifteenth of the month. It is poor planning to have a mailing piece arrive when family finances are at a low ebb.

Even the weather is an important factor in timing the release of mail. For example, one should avoid if possible the sending of advertising when the weather is stormy. This is especially applicable to outdoor entertainments. People somehow feel that the kind of weather they are having when they get the announcement will be like the weather at the time of the show. One manager of outdoor entertainment who sent out mail during a prolonged storm estimated that his returns were cut by 35 per cent because of the weather factor. If the announcement had reached the customer on a bright, sunny day, he would have sent his order immediately; but since it came with a storm, he laid it aside to be taken care of sometime later; and therein lay the danger. There is no denying that weather has a strong effect on people's moods.

CATHOLIC UNIVERSITY THEATRE

invites you to subscribe

to its

SEASON
of
FIVE PLAYS

including

THE BEST OF THE PAST

Shakespeare

Chekhov

Sophocles

...AND...

Subscription Information

FORMER SUBSCRIBERS

By filling out the attached form and mailing it to us by October 3 with a check for the amount indicated, former subscribers may renew their *same seat—same evening* subscriptions of last season. If a change of evening is requested, original seats cannot be guaranteed. After October 4th, unrenewed seats will be assigned to new subscribers.

NEW SUBSCRIBERS

New subscriptions will be assigned after October 4th. Allocation of seats will be based on the order in which applications are received at the University Theatre.

Seating Arrangements:

Subscribers select the night of the week they wish to attend for the entire season and come on the same night of the week to each play and occupy the same seats each time.

Location:

Plays are presented at the University Theatre located on the Catholic University Campus. Entrance to the campus is at Fourth Street and Michigan Avenue, N.E., easily accessible by bus or streetcar. For more specific directions, please call Michigan 6000, extension 351.

Conditions of Subscription:

Because of their reduced rate, no refunds are made on Subscription Tickets.

Subscription seats are good only on the dates indicated on tickets. Exchanges will positively not be made from one play to another. Exchanges may be made within the run of each show provided tickets are presented at the Box Office twenty-four hours in advance of date on ticket.

Exchanges cannot be made by telephone. The actual tickets must be returned to the University Theatre.

Exchanged tickets will be mailed *only* upon receipt of self-addressed, stamped envelope.

The Plays and the Dates of Performance:

1. **The Tempest**
   A fantastic, lyrical comedy
   by WILLIAM SHAKESPEARE
   OCTOBER 26-NOVEMBER 10

2. *The Cherry Orchard*
   A gentle rueful comedy
   by ANTON CHEKHOV
   NOVEMBER 30-DECEMBER 15

3. *The Cresent Moon*
   A mock-romantic comedy
   by JOHN T. DUGAN
   FEBRUARY 8-FEBRUARY 23

4. **Antigone**
   A triumphant Greek drama
   by SOPHOCLES
   MARCH 21-APRIL 5

5. **Musical Comedy**
   thirteenth annual production
   MAY 9-MAY 24

☆ ☆ ☆

OPENING NIGHT—FRIDAY. NO SUNDAY PERFORMANCES.

.. The Promise of the Future

TWO NEW PLAYS
first time anywhere

★ *A satirical swash-buckling comedy*

★ *The 13th annual Spring Musical Play—
   to be presented in association with the
   University Department of Music*

☆ ☆ ☆

A SEASON SUBSCRIPTION ASSURES SAVINGS AND SERVICE

Season subscriptions are sold at a reduced rate.
Subscribers are assured of preferred seating.
Tickets are mailed prior to the opening of each play.

RATES

Two seats for each of five productions $15.00
One seat for each of five productions . . . . . . $ 7.50

CATHOLIC UNIVERSITY THEATRE
Washington 17, D. C.
GENTLEMEN:

Please enter my subscription as follows:

NAME_____
ADDRESS_____
CITY_____PHONE NUMBER_____
AMOUNT ENCLOSED_____NUMBER OF SEATS_____
NIGHT DESIRED_____SECOND CHOICE_____
IS THIS RENEWAL _____UNDER SAME NAME_____

*Please enclose self-addressed, stamped envelope for return of subscription
card and tickets to first play.*

FIG. 9.

Catholic University Theatre uses an 8½" x 10" sheet folded to make four pages which give complete and concise information, including an order blank, statement of policy, and other important information. This is a model of simplicity and completeness. It gets results!

FIG. 10.

This mailing piece has proved to be highly successful. It is also distributed widely as a handbill. The ballet plays to over ten thousand people in five performances. This circular is one of the principal media of promotion of the show.

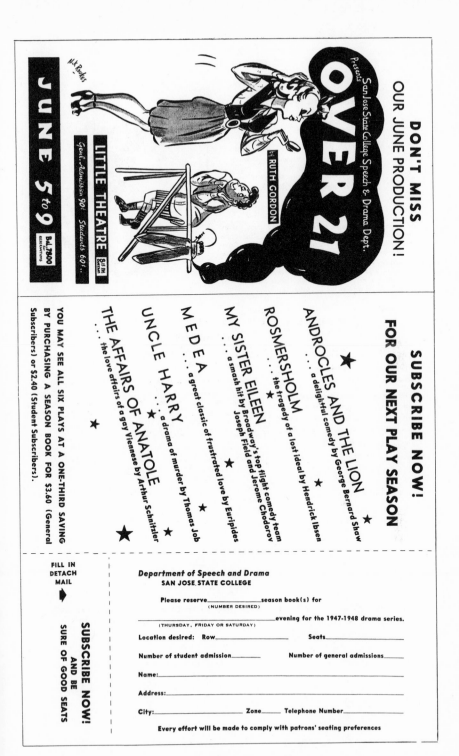

FIG. 11.

San Jose State College, Speech and Drama Department, presents a season of charm and variety. The compactness and clarity make an effective mailing piece.

The Theater Arts Department
Of U.C.L.A.

PRESENTS

A MIDSUMMER NIGHT'S DREAM

with Mendelssohn's music
Matinees at 2:50 P.M.
Student Matinee Thursday, May 29.
Regular Matinee Friday, May 30

Evenings at 8:30 P.M.
May 28, 29, 30, and 31.

As a special reduction to schools, clubs, and organizations, the popular group ticket plan will be continued. This means that groups will be able to save 50% on each ticket. There are only two requirements: tickets must be ordered before noon May 27 and in blocks of 15 or more. The rates for individual tickets purchased in the block are 25c for the matinees and 50c for the evenings. Orders received after May 23 will be held at the box office.

A MIDSUMMER NIGHT'S DREAM

GROUP ORDER

No group tickets will be sold in blocks of less than 15.

Orders received after May 23 will be held at the Royce Hall box office. No group ticket orders will be accepted after noon, *May 27.*

The Concert Series Ticket Office is located at

10851 Le Conte Ave.
Los Angeles 24
BRadshaw 2-6161
or
ARizona 3-0971
Extension 379

Concert Series Ticket Office
University of California
University Extension
Los Angeles 24, California

You will find my check/money order in the amount of $_____.

Please send me_____tickets at 25c each for the matinee performance of_____(specify Thursday, May 29, or Friday, May 30.) and/or_____tickets at 50c each for the evening performance of_____ _____(specify Wednesday, May 28, Thursday, May 29, Friday, May 30, or Saturday, May 31.)

(Please make checks payable to the Regents of the University of California)

Name_____
Address_____
School, Club, or Organization_____
_____Phone_____

FIG. 12.

This is a group order form for one play. It features attractive prices and courteous service. The information is complete in the fewest possible words.

FIG. 13.

This is one of many clever bits of advertising devised by Director Horace Robinson of the University of Oregon.

WAYNE STATE UNIVERSITY THEATRE
1956-57 Season Subscription Order

7 PLAYS FOR $5.00   or   **4 PLAYS FOR $4.00**

See each of the 7 plays and save over 40%   Choose any 4 of the 7 and save 20%

(Individual Tickets are $1.25)

Check boxes for desired plays and dates.

	FRI.	SAT.	THURS.	FRI.	SAT.	SUN.
1. THE GREAT GOD BROWN by Eugene O'Neill	Oct. 12 ☐	Oct. 13 ☐	Oct. 18 ☐	Oct. 19 ☐	Oct. 20 ☐	No Performance
2. AN ITALIAN STRAW HAT by Labiche and Michel	Nov. 9 ☐	Nov. 10 ☐	Nov. 15 ☐	Nov. 16 ☐	Nov. 17 ☐	No Performance
3. THE FATHER by August Strindberg	Dec. 7 ☐	Dec. 8 ☐	Dec. 13 ☐	Dec. 14 ☐	Dec. 15 ☐	No Performance
4. THIEVES' CARNIVAL by Jean Anouilh	Feb. 8 ☐	Feb. 9 ☐	Feb. 14 ☐	Feb. 15 ☐	Feb. 16 ☐	No Performance
5. THE BEAUTIFUL PEOPLE by William Saroyan	Mar. 1 ☐	Mar. 2 ☐	Mar. 7 ☐	Mar. 8 ☐	Mar. 9 ☐	No Performance
6. THE TEMPEST by William Shakespeare	Apr. 5 ☐	Apr. 6 ☐	Apr. 11 ☐	Apr. 12 ☐	Apr. 13 ☐	No Performance
7. SPRING DANCE CONCERT with THE MAN WHO MARRIED A DUMB WIFE by Anatole France	No Performance	No Performance	May 16 ☐	May 17 ☐	May 18 ☐	May 19 ☐

Curtain time -- 8:30 p.m., except for the Sunday performance, which is 3:00 p.m.

FOR THE STUDENT-STAFF RATE (7 PLAYS FOR $3.00), BRING ORDER AND ACTIVITY BOOK TO TICKET OFFICE
Eligible: Wayne students, full-time staff members, and husbands or wives of full-time staff members

Mail to: Wayne State University Ticket Office
　　　　　Room 208 Old Main
　　　　　Detroit 2, Michigan

FOR TICKET OFFICE USE
Order No._____
Location_____

Please reserve for me_____season tickets at $_____each for 1956-57 as checked above. Enclosed please find $_____
to cover ticket price, and a STAMPED, SELF-ADDRESSED ENVELOPE for return of the tickets.

Name_____

Address_____

City_____Zone_____Telephone_____

☐ I am not interested in season tickets but I would appreciate an announcement of each play.

Make checks payable to Wayne State University

FIG. 14.

Although this brochure has no decorative features, it is complete and
accurate in every detail. Notice that the order blank is separate so that
the patron may keep the announcement and return the order.

VIII

EVERYBODY READS THE NEWSPAPERS

Sweet are the uses of publicity. For long centuries the ubiquitous newspapers have been regarded by show people as the most effective and most powerful over-all medium for the entertainment world. Theatres of both yesterday and today have been tremendously dependent upon the press. Without its strong support, a theatre is in a precarious position; but given such support and with a program that has public appeal, it has a good chance to survive, even to prosper. Readers rely upon newspapers for authoritative information regarding everything from prices of admission to critics' evaluations. "What does the paper say?" is a question that settles other questions.

The public relations aspect of dealing with the press is extremely important. Criticizing the paper and constantly complaining about its comments may work for a short time, but it is a dangerous practice. The promoter must supply the editor with a variety of stories. Do not expect busy reporters to come to you—they are looking for news that is more sensational and broader in nature. Furthermore, the editor is likely to object to your trying to turn his sacred sheet into an advertising circular. Newspaper men may not all be geniuses, but they have no trouble in telling the difference between a news story and an advertising essay. Some theatre managers have complained that the press gives them no support, only complete indifference. In such a case, it is time to make a careful study of the theatre-press relations. Uses of newspapers are unlimited, but the imagination and style of the writers are often stereotyped. The press agent who looks to the theatre page only as an outlet for his stories is using but 10 per cent of his press power. During a theatre season almost every section of the entire paper might be made available. The theatre can often find new readers by breaking into new columns and departments where theatre stories are not usually found. Lest we forget, editors are constantly on the lookout for interesting copy which their readers will enjoy. To supply this will require exploration of all divisions of the paper.

With the idea of widening the base of operations, let us take a preliminary look at the various sections of the newspaper: (1) theatre page, (2) local news, (3) society section, (4) editorial page, (5) local and syndicated columns, (6) special features, (7) sports pages, and (8) church section. It is obvious that few plays will have a sufficiently wide appeal to be of interest to all sections of a newspaper, but each play presented should be carefully weighed for its publicity values. A spark of imagination, a new twist or novel approach may make all the difference in the world. Let us review some of the possibilities of the newspaper.

1. *The theatre page* is the most obvious spot for drama stories as well as for paid advertising. It is the strongest most certain connection with the public. Almost everyone who checks on what is offered, time, locations, and prices, automatically goes to that page. Consequently this space is always at a premium. Advertising and publicity agents for movies and concerts seek to obtain attention with unremitting perseverance. There is never a letdown in the competition for space. Often your promotion man will be disappointed to see that his story has been cut, the picture has been taken out, or the entire story has been deleted —and this may have happened when you most needed it. In such cases the only thing to do is to come right back with other stories and different angles—do everything possible to get back in the game. Don't scold; don't nag.

In planning a series of stories for the theatre page, try to get them in proper sequence. The first story may concern the announcement of dates, tryouts, names of plays, and later the cast. It is a strange fact that the newspaper is always asking for the cast of characters; but when you have given them the cast, they seem to think everything is finished; they say, in effect, "What else is there? We've already run the cast." To an editor, the story of the cast is the last possible thing that could be written before the show. It is good policy not to throw everything in at once, but to keep feeding it in smaller articles. A short article with a good picture is much more desirable than a long article with no picture.

Except for members of the immediate theatre family, it's hard to find people who will read a long story, but everyone will look at a picture and the caption.

2. *The local news* will often carry interesting stories concerning general development of the theatre, new plans, new faces, personnel, and improvements, provided that they come at times other than just before the show. If such stories are offered immediately before the show, the editor may have a haunting suspicion that his precious columns are being sought for advertising purposes, and this he will regard as a misuse of the press. However, he may feel favorable when the pressure is off. A story of redecoration of the theatre, new personnel, plans for the new season, or changes of policy may be welcome. If such stories are periodically sent to the editor, he will eventually find space. Fortune Gallo, famous impresario of the San Carlo Opera Company, made it his business to send in pictures with short articles, pictures with long articles, medium-sized articles, and sometimes just a picture with a little caption. Gallo's belief was that if you keep at this unfailingly, the breaks will come and you'll get exactly what you want.

3. *The society page* has a special interest group. Some localities are much more susceptible to this angle in the theatre than others. Here is a division of publicity that requires a person of special talents to work the angles properly. It is easy to overplay it so that the great public will say, "Well, this thing seems to be aimed at the society people; let society people support it."

It has been the policy of most symphony organizations throughout the country to lean rather heavily on this section of the newspaper. The standard formula is to have a big meeting and invite the best-known society people. Though the meeting is actually a drive, it is not called that. Names and faces will now appear in the proper section of the newspaper. Subsequently, there will be another picture and story of society people arriving at the concert. Often a microphone is strategically set up where guests may tell the public how thrilled they are to be attending the first night. The third step is to have a big reception after the initial performance.

Sometimes effective publicity is obtained by having parties for the stars, the staff, or the patrons of the theatre. Some communities report the society page to be highly effective while in others the use of the society page is negligible.

4. *The editorial page* is the gold mine of the newspaper which is often overlooked. Community leaders, thinkers, teachers, and scholars, as well as many of the public, take the reading of the editorial page rather seriously. If the press is in sympathy with your theatre or entertainment venture, it will not be difficult to get an editorial. If you will take the trouble to furnish the editors with the facts about your theatre, such as its influence and place in the community, its growth and development, they will write the editorial. In some communities managers are able to justify several laudatory editorials a season. It might well be that your theatre is not giving to the community the quality of service it should give and that the Theatre Board should look to a better program and thereby win a better support of the press. The important thing is that when something is done by the theatre for the benefit of the community, the press should be encouraged to write it up.

Another feature of the editorial page is the letters to the editor section. These have unlimited possibilities, but they also have dangers. Almost every newspaper has a section for letters variously referred to as "What Our Readers Think," "The Public Pulse," or "Letters to the Editor." These are usually short and crisp. A favorable letter can be helpful, but what often happens is that some irate person who does not represent the attitude of the community at all writes a strong letter criticizing the show for its profanity, bad situations, or its straight talk, while thousands of people who really enjoyed the entertainment and were not the least offended never write a word. It is concerning this silent group that action should be taken. If someone calls on the phone or comes to the office all excited about the theatre's unjust criticism, get him to write a letter of reply right now. Furnish him paper and stamp, and address the envelope to the editor. Get the letter in the mail. There certainly is nothing wrong with having people report their good opinions about your show. The press will be willing to print both sides of the story. You're not asking anyone to misrepresent his thoughts, but merely to put in writing what he has told you. Here is a sample of the kind of comment which every theatre producer has heard and perhaps has not capitalized on:

DEAR EDITOR:

We recently moved to your city from another state. Last night my husband and I attended the Kalamazoo Civic Theatre. It was one of the most wonderful experiences we have ever had. We were delighted to note the enthusiasm of the audience, and we wondered if all the citizens of the town knew what a

wonderful cultural opportunity the theatre presented. Where we lived before there was no civic theatre, and we missed that feature a great deal. Here the citizens have the opportunity of seeing the best at a very reasonable price, and we just thought we ought to write in and let you know how we feel about this.
Sincerely yours,

Even unfavorable letters may set off a chain reaction which will create more public interest than you could imagine. For instance, when one summer theatre presented *South Pacific* several letters were published screaming about the profanity and some of the sexy situations. Immediately other people wrote letters pointing out that such objections to a great show were childish and provincial. The fight was on, and the result was a busines pickup at the box office because everybody wanted to see if the dangerous show was sexy or harmful to morals. Criticisms either strongly in favor or strongly against your show will get public response. Reports which are tepid have little value.

5. *Local column* writers are always on the lookout for an interesting anecdote, a fresh story, or a spicy bit. Usually these columnists are widely read and this unplanned publicity is most welcome. One writer featured the fact that ballet dancers wear out a pair of expensive shoes in about five or six performances. He described the size and appearance of the ballet slippers. In another case someone was ill and a faithful understudy stepped in and did a magnificent job. Stories of unsung heroes in amateur as well as professional performances are legion.

Humorous incidents and stage mishaps are common to all theatres. Some of them are extremely amusing. One director reported that once his lighting cues got crossed so that when the leading lady, looking skyward, said, "Is there anything more beautiful than a full moon rising?" she was greeted with thunder and lightning; and when the storm was supposed to be raging, the moon came up and all was serene. To a director such things are tragic, but the audience laughs them off.

Animals in shows will furnish human-interest stories. There is a story possibility concerning the goat in *Teahouse of the August Moon,* another about the dog in *The Barretts of Wimpole Street.* There is no trouble getting such items into the columns of local writers; they are waiting for them. All that is necessary is a little ingenuity and one mouse power of effort to write them up.

6. *The syndicated columns* may be more interested in your particular story than the local writers. Sending your story or your question may

help not only you, but it may be of great interest and assistance to other theatres. It is worth a try.

Ann Landers might be interested in the following lament because she has answered similar questions.

DEAR ANN LANDERS:

For the past several months, my husband has been spending his evenings out with other men; and he seldom invites me to go with him. He used to tell me he enjoyed going out with me. He goes to the wrestling matches or to the bowling alleys. When I asked him why he didn't take me along, he merely said, "Oh, you wouldn't enjoy that stuff." I tried to get him to go to the theatre and the orchestra concerts, but he said that he could not stand them and that they were patronized by a lot of stuffed shirts. Now, I love these cultural things and I want to go, but I don't want to go alone. Across the street from us, there is a friend whose wife died last summer. He indicated that he would be glad to take me along any time to the theatre or concert because he often went anyway. Would it be proper for me to accept such invitations? After all, I feel that I am entitled to some enjoyment, and I want to attend some cultural programs. Please give me your frank opinion.

7. *The feature page* is a natural for the theatre because every dramatic production is a new adventure. Successful special features have been done on "How a Show is Lighted"; "The Importance and the Application of Stage Make-Up," by transforming a young girl through the various steps of becoming an old woman; or "How Scenery is Prepared for a Big Production"; and, of course "Backstage at Dress Rehearsal"; or "Costuming a Big Production." The good feature writer requires only ingenuity and imagination to come up with an angle that is worthy.

Even the home life of actors and theatre people is interesting to the public. Charles Prickett, formerly manager of the Pasadena Playhouse, was well known for his ingenious creation of household conveniences and novelties, and this hobby made an exciting newspaper feature. Recently, a recipe book was brought out showing the favorite recipes of different musicians. It answered the question that many people ask: "What do these people eat? How do they live, and how do they like to be entertained in private life?" National magazines are continually featuring intimate stories of the lives of stage personalities.

One last word regarding the feature story: it must be given to someone who knows what to do with it; otherwise, you may get stupid comments and pictures which will only embarrass the people whom you intended to honor.

8. *Sports page*. Because sports are able to get ample space when nothing else can, it is often easy to promote a story about the theatre if it can tie in with some sport. For example, when a children's theatre persuaded a 6-foot 10-inch basketball center to play the giant in *Jack and the Beanstalk,* a picture and story of considerable size were printed. The young people, especially the boys, were anxious to see the show with their basketball hero. Certain plays, such as *Golden Boy* and *The Champion* are built around dramatic moments of sports. The fact that Victor Jory was once a championship boxer made it easy to place a picture showing him giving tips to young boxers—presenting a new angle of his life which might otherwise never have been known. Actors skilled in skiing, golf, tennis, basketball, swimming, wrestling, fencing, and baseball can furnish excellent material for the sports page, and thus may make new friends for the theatre, who would not ordinarily have been reached through any other medium.

9. *The church section* is often overlooked. Many followers of these pages will be surprised and delighted to know that your theatre is presenting plays with strong religious messages or implications. You will thus reach another group with a potential theatre interest. There are quite a number of religious plays. Two modern ones which have proved highly successful are *The Vigil,* which is especially appropriate for Easter, and *The Family Portrait,* which is often presented as a Christmas play. Both of these are well written and have universal appeal, thus standing to gain theatre patrons among churches of all faiths. Moreover, the inclusion of an occasional religious play in a schedule indicates breadth of interest and an awareness of the theatre's responsibility to the community. Support or lack of support of the churches may easily spell the difference between success or failure of your theatre.

Preparation of the Newspaper Story

How carefully should the newspaper story be written? Who should write it? Why not just telephone it in? Won't the newspaper send out a reporter? Why don't we get better support from the press? These are the questions which amateur theatre people ask of each other; but if they would ask the press, the answer might be something like this:

All stories should be typed, double spaced on 8½″ × 11″ white paper. There should be ample margins on sides, top and bottom, which make it possible to insert corrections and alterations. The copy should be clean and not marred with erasures and strike-overs. Many newspapers have a little book on "Rules of Style" which can be very helpful.

If there are two or more newspapers in your community, it is most important that you do not send them the same story and identical pictures. If newspapers were identical, there would be no need to have more than one. To an editor, a carbon copy of a story is a sort of red flag, telling him that you have given the identical item to other papers and that he is in second place. Some facts of a story must, of course, be identical but the angle of approach as well as the beginning and conclusion should be different if you expect to get your story published. If ever you break faith with an editor by sending him a duplicate story, you may find it difficult to get back in his good graces. The old proverb, "Once suspicion enters the human heart, it never leaves," does not exempt newspaper editors.

Needless to say, copy should be sent in when it is news. Publishers are understandably hesitant about printing anything that smells like "old stuff." Hence, one of the theatre promoter's most difficult problems is that of making his material seem fresh and interesting.

The right word is important in the preparation of promotion stories or advertising matter. The writer should have among his tools a full reserve of accurate and colorful words and phrases. These not only furnish him the adjectives he needs, but they stimulate his imagination and accelerate his thinking. Mark Twain said, "The difference in the choice of the right word and almost the right word is the difference between lightning and the lightning bug." Joseph Conrad said, "The use of the right word is more important than the right argument." "We rule men with words," said Napoleon. Every play cannot be "colossal," "unexcelled," or "stupendous." It is often much easier to select the right word from a list than it is to dredge it up from one's own word supply. A good dictionary or a dictionary of synonyms will always be helpful, but the limited list of adjectives on page 87, may suggest ideas for the writer of publicity and advertising.

How to deliver the publicity story may be an important consideration. If at all possible, a special messenger of the publicity manager himself should deliver the story to the press. The messenger as well as the message may be important. Occasionally a special delivery letter will do very well. Regular mail is not especially impressive. Of course, the main thing is that the story should reach the hands of the one responsible for

absorbing	exclusive	jaunty	primitive	unexcelled
action-packed	exhilarating	jolly	pungent	unexpurgated
adult	exotic	jovial	puzzling	unique
amazing		jubilant		unorthodox
angelic	fabulous		quaint	unparalleled
animated	famous	keen	quick	uplifting
artistic	fancy			
attractive	fantastic	laughable	racy	versatile
authentic	farcical	lavish	refreshing	victorious
awesome	fascinating	legitimate	remarkable	vigorous
	fast-moving	lively	revealing	violent
benevolent	frivolous	lofty	rewarding	visionary
bizarre	full-blooded	logical	risqué	vital
blood-chilling	fun-filled	lovely	roaring	vivacious
booming	funny	ludicrous	romantic	vivid
bouncy		lurid		
brilliant	gala	lyric	scintillating	warm
bubbly	genuine		sensational	well-arranged
buoyant	ghastly	magnificent	sentimental	well-balanced
	ghostlike	majestic	sexy	well-chosen
celebrated	gigantic	malevolent	sidesplitting	well-known
charming	gorgeous	marvelous	shocking	well-timed
chilling	graphic	masterful	simple	well-told
classic	greatest	melodic	sinister	whimsical
colorful	gripping	melodramatic	sleazy humor	wholesome
comic	grisly	memorable	smash hit	winning
compelling		merry	sparkling	wistful
constructive	hard-hitting	modern	spectacular	witty
"cool"	heartwarming	moving	spellbinding	wonderful
courageous	heavenly		spicy	wondrous
curious	hidden	new	spooky	
	hilarious	nerve-tingling	startling	zany
dazzling	historical	notable	stimulating	zestful
delightful	homely	notorious	stirring	zippy
devilish	homespun	novel	strong	
different	horrible		stupendous	
dignified	humorous	original	sublime	
distinguished	hypnotic	orthodox	subtle	
diverting		outspoken	superior	
drama-packed	illustrious	outstanding	swift-moving	
dramatic	imaginative	overwhelming		
dynamic	impressive		tantalizing	
	incisive	passionate	tender	
eerie	incredible	penetrating	terrific	
effective	infamous	peppy	thought-provoking	
effervescent	inimitable	perfect	thrilling	
elevating	inspiring	phenomenal	throbbing	
eloquent	intense	poetic	topnotch	
emotional	intimate	poignant	traditional	
enthralling	inviting	polished	tragic	
entertaining		popular	tremendous	
exciting	jarring	powerful	true	

FIG. 15.

88

seeing that it gets into print on time. If such a story has to pass through a number of irresponsible hands, as it sometimes does, anything can happen to it. The futility as well as the impossibility of tracking down a lost story is something one learns from experience. Precaution is better.

Finally, it is highly important that proper invitations with tickets to see the show be extended to the people of the press who have assisted you in publicity stories and reviews. Such invitations should be gracious and sincere. You may not always feel like being kind to the press, but it is the better way. After all, they have the last word.

Paid Newspaper Advertising

The paid advertisement in the newspaper has long been regarded by professional showmen as the most important medium and the one where most of the advertising money should be spent. They argue that people depend on this for authentic information—the final word. Records of managers and promoters indicate that more than 90 per cent of the advertising money goes to this medium. Many newspapers will not run stories about theatres or plays unless paid advertising is run also. A few have a policy of printing stories whether or not advertising space is purchased. To say the least, the fact that paid advertising is in may help the cause; certainly it won't hurt.

A Broadway show's opening night will be advertised in the leading New York papers, with the name of the show, time, place, prices, box office location, dates, and sometimes the names of stars. Because space in these metropolitan newspapers is extremely expensive the size of subsequent advertisements must be minimum and the show doing good box office or it will quickly reach the point of diminishing returns.

Newspaper advertising space is usually sold by the column inch—that is, a block 1 inch deep and 1 column wide, or approximately 2 square inches. An advertisement 2 columns wide by 7 inches deep would occupy a total of 14 column inches. On the other hand, many large newspapers quote space charges by the "line." Since there are 14 lines to an inch, at a rate of $2 per line a column inch would cost $28. If a show bought a 1-inch advertisement in eight New York papers it could cost over $200.

Fortunately, since most educational and civic theatres are in smaller cities, they do not have to worry about such high rates, but neither do they reach the millions of people. Rates are based on certified circulation figures, and some of the big New York dailies run into the millions. Show-business advertisers try to get the maximum return for newspaper dollars. Copy should be carefully planned and so organized that the reader can get all facts at a glance. Although everyone expects to find all theatre advertisements on the entertainment page with other theatrical displays, newspapers often suggest that it might be well to place a theatre advertisement on some other page if their space demands are especially heavy. Yet studies show that your advertisement will lose 90 per cent of its effectiveness if it is placed on any other page. People get in the habit of looking for things in certain places. For example, all want advertisements go in a certain section and are further classified and indexed within the "want ad" section.

Little illustrative pictures, commonly referred to as "mats" or "cuts," often dress up an advertisement. Sometimes these may be obtained from the newspaper itself, sometimes from an advertising service. It is well to look over what is available, or to consult some advertising service. Package Publicity Service, 247 West 46th Street, New York 36, New York, can give assistance on a number of popular plays. It would be advisable to write for this information. Full details, including a list of plays which have prepared information can be obtained upon request, and the service is excellent.

Many theatres use distinctive trade-marks on their advertisements such as a pair of masks, the pillars of the theatre, or a draped proscenium arch. Cornell University uses an impressive line drawing of a woman's face. It is well to have a good artist prepare a symbol or trademark which will represent your theatre everywhere. (The Coca-Cola Company is an example of an organization that has made the most of such a simple symbol.)

Advertising space should always be requisitioned early, and clean copy and layout prepared in time to get proof from which to make corrections and changes. Because newspaper workers are constantly fighting deadlines, the service which they can give is limited. If they have the copy on time, they can dummy it on the page and supply the proofs for corrections and changes. It occasionally happens that space on the theatre page is not even available for last minute requests. This may cause bitter disappointments and even hardships for the show. On the other hand, space which is ordered in advance may be released if it is not needed. In short, it is much easier to alter a plan than not to have one at all. A letter requesting space might read as follows:

DEAR SIR:

The ——— theatre requests you to reserve advertising space on the amusement page as follows:

Sunday,	Jan. 8,	2 columns by	7"	or 14"
Wednesday,	Feb. 7,	2 columns by	4"	or 8"
Thursday,	Feb. 9,	2 columns by	4"	or 8"
Friday,	Feb. 10,	2 columns by	4"	or 8"
Saturday,	Feb. 11,	2 columns by	2"	or 4"
			Total	42"

Your order number is ——. Copy for the first insertion on Sunday, January 8 is enclosed. Other copy will be furnished as needed. We would like to have all advertisements appear on the amusement page with other theatrical advertising. It would be appreciated if our advertisement could be placed at the top of the page next to reading matter.

It will be necessary for us to see the proof of each advertisement before it is printed.

Sincerely,

The following page shows an advertising layout with appropriate markings which may offer helpful suggestions:

This advertisement was set up from the information supplied by the theatre.

If the advertiser is not well acquainted with types and sizes, it will be easier to use a percentage system to indicate proportions. For instance, the largest type of this page is 1/2″ tall and bold; this could be marked 100 per cent and then 50, 25, 10, and so on. It would give the printer some idea of what is wanted.

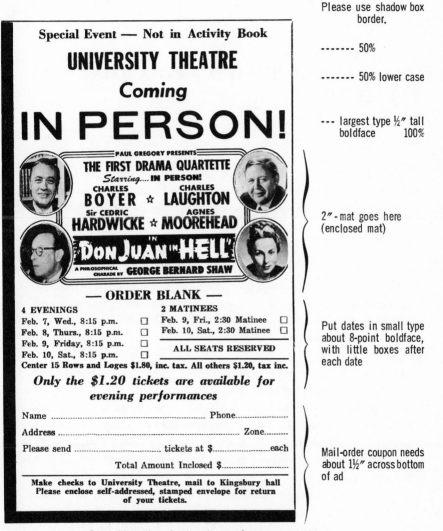

Please use shadow box border.

------- 50%

------- 50% lower case

--- largest type ½″ tall boldface   100%

2″ - mat goes here (enclosed mat)

Put dates in small type about 8-point boldface, with little boxes after each date

Mail-order coupon needs about 1½″ across bottom of ad

Date of insertion: Sunday, January 8, on amusement page.
Size: 2 columns by 7 inches. Proof requested.

FIG. 16.

IX

SEVEN OTHER TESTED MEDIA THAT SELL THE SHOW

The wisdom of the bearded adage about beating a trail to the man with the best mousetrap may be questioned today. It was never a very good proverb and the only theatres that ever believed it, even in the good old days, have gone out of business.

Theatre Posters and Posting

"The best does not cost any more anymore." In a world of keen entertainment competition, the living theatre must obtain a sufficient number of effective posters and put them in the choicest spots. Anything less than a first-class job will fall into the category of "too little and too late."

The custom of posting window cards, one-sheets, three-sheets, and twenty-four-sheets, plus a miscellaneous lot of other shapes and sizes is still an important part of show business. Competition has made it necessary to brighten up the poster program and to think of "hidden persuaders" as well as those which are obvious and bare faced. There is no rule of thumb to tell one just how effective his posters are, or just what kind and how many to use. But there are a few basic principles which, if applied with common sense, should help to get people into the theatre —which is the purpose of the poster, whether it is the size of a campaign button or a street banner. It should go without saying that theatre posters should be attractive and not cluttered by too much detail. How many posters should a theatre use? Well, here is an old formula which is much better than nothing and has worked for many advertisers:

150 window cards	6 twenty-four-sheets
20 one-sheets	2,000 handbills or circulars
10 three-sheets	24 photographs of cast, etc.

One can cut down or add according to the needs. If there is no place to put some of these items, it would, of course, be useless to order them, but you might find a place.

The next thing is to consult an expert in the poster field. A letter to any one of the following poster printers will produce prices and helpful suggestions. It is an excellent idea to write to more than one. Most of these firms carry a variety of attractive borders and colored stock, and they have type faces to suit the assignment. Best of all, their work is well done and the service is excellent. There may be local printers who can do the work well and inexpensively, but it is a good idea to explore a little.

Bell Press, Winton, Pennsylvania.

Consolidated Lithographers, Glencove and Vine Roads, Carle Place, New York.

Compton and Sons, Inc., 216 South Seventh, St. Louis, Missouri.

National Printers and Engravers, 7 South Dearborn, Chicago, Illinois.

Progress Lithographing Co., Section Road and Prr., Cincinnati, Ohio.

Posters, Inc., 835 Cherry St., Philadelphia, Pennsylvania.

The Enquirer Printing Co., 412 East Sixth Street, Cincinnati 2, Ohio.

A few theatres are fortunate enough to have a good artist and a silk-screen expert who can take care of the poster problem economically. But even so, it might be worthwhile to seek a little variety and some new ideas.

One of the most effective window cards is one made up with a bordered space left open to paste in an 8″ × 10″ photograph of members of the cast. These are real eye-catchers; and although they cost from sixty to eighty cents, they are worth it if you place them in good locations. Window cards and other posters with a cartoon, an animal, a house, a tree, or a caricature suggesting the play will add to the interest. Even the plain card which merely tells its story has a place because repetition is still a feature of advertising.

If your theatre has not used one-sheets and three-sheets, they might be worth a try. A one-sheet is equal in area to four $14'' \times 22''$ window cards and a three-sheet is equal to twelve of them. In good positions they are certainly twelve times as strong as the cards.

In ordering posters it is well to calculate carefully the number which can be used effectively, plus a few extras for replacements. Furthermore, if one looks around circumspectly, he may find that some good spots have been overlooked. Following the same old routine does not require any imagination or thinking; anyone can do that.

Posting. It is not enough that the theatre have attractive posters; they should be put up in conspicuous spots where people will surely see them. Nor is putting them up a job for just anybody who is out of work; it is a job for someone who is interested and who really cares. If this important final step is poorly done, the project is lost; if it is well done, it will pay well. Here is an important assignment in public relations that should be handled with dignity and tact. The best posting results will be obtained by sending out a well-dressed young man and young woman who are thoroughly prepared for the assignment and who can speak effectively. They should be trained representatives of the theatre, who will visit managers or someone in charge of advertising in stores, shops, banks, cafes, hotels, and offices. Who asks whom is an important part of the sale. The appearance of the messenger may be as important as the messages. If the manager knows that he is talking to people who understand his problems as well as their own, and if he finds that the theatre cares enough about his good will to send respectable representatives, he may be receptive.

Let us suppose that it is the beginning of the theatre season, and the appointed young man and young woman, who know what they are doing, go to the store and ask to see the manager. They do not discuss their problem with the man at the door, or the secretary, or the janitor—they go to the top. After they have explained their request, the manager will probably approve the idea and introduce them to the one who will take care of putting the cards in the windows. The theatre people can assist, both with suggestions and with actually placing the cards, having ready the necessary tape, tacks or whatever is needed to get the job completed. Posters should not be left to be put up later—not more than one in ten will ever put up the posters later. The reason for this failure is not that people mean to deceive, but they have other things to do. Once your work is tabled it can easily get lost forever. When making a request, it is better to ask, "How many cards can you use?" rather than, "Can you use any cards?" Always arrange a choice between something and something else rather than a choice between something and nothing: "To put up one poster or more than one poster," rather than "To put up the poster or not to put up the poster," that is the question. If the approach to the downtown people is on a high plane it will probably be well received. It all depends upon the type of people who do the work and the approach they use. So much for the downtown poster business.

Around the campus the problems are much the same. Those in charge of putting up posters must find suitable spots. Usually the regular bulletin boards are so jammed with junk that the poster is lost as soon as you add it to the clutter. What does one do? Find new places; make new places. Maybe it would pay the theatre to locate or build some three-sheet boards of its own. Is there a conspicuous corner that can be utilized at small cost? It is a good idea to get acquainted with the janitor and persuade him to help you find some good locations. Give him some tickets to the theatre; if you get him working with you he won't disturb your posters. You can ask him to take them down as soon as the show is over. Janitors and custodians are often a bit exacting because they are not treated with respect. A bit of recognition and courtesy will get them on your team, and they can help you a great deal. "A little honey will catch more flies than a lot of vinegar."

No one can blame you for wanting your show to succeed. It may be well to explain to the authorities that you cannot operate theatre advertising as if the theatre were the FBI. If you think so, take a look at the billboards along the highways. After all, the school or theatre cannot expect you to get publicity if you have to work secretly. Usually the administrative officers who make the rules know that you can't operate in secrecy, and they're quite willing to be a little lenient.

The limited samples which follow are typical of what might be used to make up window cards and larger posters such as one-sheets and three sheets. It is common policy to prepare attractive copy and let it serve several uses. Most of the advertising, of course, makes use of colors. Handbills, usually $6'' \times 9''$, carry advertising, such as newspaper comments and mail order forms. This is an effective medium because thousands can be distributed inexpensively.

FIG. 17.

FIG. 18.

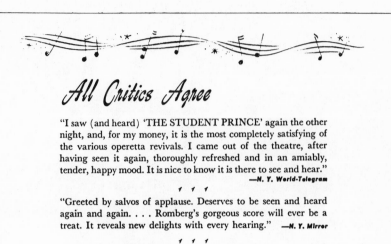

All Critics Agree

"I saw (and heard) 'THE STUDENT PRINCE' again the other night, and, for my money, it is the most completely satisfying of the various operetta revivals. I came out of the theatre, after having seen it again, thoroughly refreshed and in an amiably, tender, happy mood. It is nice to know it is there to see and hear."
—*N. Y. World-Telegram*

♪ ♪ ♪

"Greeted by salvos of applause. Deserves to be seen and heard again and again. . . . Romberg's gorgeous score will ever be a treat. It reveals new delights with every hearing." —*N. Y. Mirror*

♪ ♪ ♪

"A harmonious delight . . . restful, simple, satisfying . . . as handsome a revival as you have any right to ask for." *N. Y. Daily News*

♪ ♪ ♪

"One fine melody follows another." —*N. Y. Times*

♪ ♪ ♪

"Still one of the most tuneful shows in town." —*N. Y. Sun*

♪ ♪ ♪

"An entertainment which you should certainly see and hear."
—*N. Y. Herald Tribune*

- -

MAIL ORDER FORM FOR "THE STUDENT PRINCE"
For your convenience—and for best locations—use this order blank
(*See reverse side for theatre prices and locations*)

Treasurer...
(Name of Theatre)

Kindly send me.........................seats for "THE STUDENT PRINCE" @ $.......................each, in the

Orchestra ☐ 1st Balcony ☐ Box ☐ (Check one) for the Matinee ☐ performance
Mezzanine ☐ 2nd Balcony ☐ Loge ☐ Evening ☐

on...Remittance for $..
(Day of week and date) (Total amount)
and a self-addressed stamped envelope are enclosed.

Name...Street and No...

City... State......................Phone................................
491

FIG. 19.

YOUR OFFICIAL INVITATION

to

ENGLEWOOD COLORADO

7 Glorious Days | 7 Glorious Nights

July 26 thru Aug. 1

Come! Celebrate!

JOIN WITH US
IN RE-LIVING OUR
50 YEARS OF PROGRESS

Program

For An Entire Week

•

Sunday, July 26
Prayer for Peace

Monday, July 27
Homecoming Day

Tuesday, July 28
Oldtimers Day

Wed., July 29
Junior Olympics Day
Boy Scout-Girl Scout-Campfire Girl Day

Thurs., July 30
Industrial Day

Friday, July 31
Agriculture Day

Saturday, Aug. 1
Colorado Day

•

FIG. 20.

Keep this away from your teachers!

Dear Student,

Stop blaming yourself; it's not your fault. It's the teachers! ... those awful people. If you were not an intelligent, likeable person, you positively would not be at this university. Remember too, *your mother loves you.*

Perhaps you're going too fast? burning yourself out? over ambitious? you want to get somewhere and fast? Say, do you know what happened to Willie Stark? Huh? He was a bright student like you. Like you he studied history, chemistry, languages, English, speech, economics, music, biology, why marry, and law. He got ideas; he started throwing ideas around. And, lo, one day he got an idea that started throwing him around. All the king's men couldn't stop what followed. He upset the university; he upset the state; he upset ... well, you better get it straight from the mouth of the horse. There's a whole unforgettable and powerful drama about Willie and you'll never forgive yourself if you miss it.

You have already bought a ticket. Look and see if you have it with you now! Yes, you have. It is coupon number 13 in your handbook and it's worth $1.20 to you.

Take that coupon to the University Theatre box office in Kingsbury Hall right now, i.e., today, and exchange it for your reserved seat ticket for "ALL THE KING'S MEN". It plays Wednesday, Thursday, Friday and Saturday, November 30, December 1, 2, and 3. Yes, yes, it is *this* week. Extra tickets are available next to yours.

Remember, you'll never forgive yourself if you miss this play!

Very sincerely yours,

Himit Knows

FIG. 21.

University Theatre *Kingsbury Hall — University of Utah*

2 MATINEES
February 9, Friday, 2:30 p.m.
February 10, Saturday, 2:30 p.m.

4 EVENINGS
February 7, Wednesday, 8:15 p.m.
February 8, Thursday, 8:15 p.m.
February 9, Friday, 8:15 p.m.
February 10, Saturday, 8:15 p.m.

ALL SEATS RESERVED
$1.80 — $1.20 (tax inc.)

PAUL GREGORY
presents
THE FIRST DRAMA QUARTETTE
Starring.. **IN PERSON!**
CHARLES BOYER
CHARLES LAUGHTON
Sir CEDRIC HARDWICKE
AGNES MOOREHEAD
in
"DON JUAN in HELL"
A PHILOSOPHICAL CHARADE BY
George Bernard Shaw

FIG. 22.

This sheet has the identical information which appeared on the window cards and larger posters—one sheet and three sheets. A lithographer or printer can either reduce or enlarge a good basic illustration.

The Telephone

Telephone campaigns are so effective for selling entertainment in some localities that the entire advertising program is conducted by this single medium. Kansas City, for example, has a successful artists series that is sold almost entirely by telephone. The campaign is handled in professional style by well-trained telephone salesmen—the organization would never think of permitting an untrained solicitor to call a prospective customer.

The fact that a few theatres can use the telephone so successfully is evidence of its power. Many promotion groups have not even understood the possibilities of this medium, much less made use of them.

There is, however, one limiting factor of the telephone campaign: after a sale has been made, there is no way by which one can collect money over the wire; the best one can do is to get a commitment. Hence, every customer must be assured that the sale is regarded as final and complete and that the buyer should send his remittance immediately. "Immediately" is a key word. The law of postponement says that the loss of sales caused by people backing out is directly proportionate to the passing of hours before payment is made. "Now is always the best time." It may be advisable to give some special incentive such as a discount, bonus, or even a cup and saucer for prompt remittance. The great human tendency is to put off doing anything and everything which is not entirely pleasant.

A telephone campaign may also be used effectively as a follow-up on a mailing list. Often people who have received the mailed announcement and who fully intend to order the tickets simply have not written the check and put it in the mail. Even the slightest reason for failure to complete the final act is just as bad for the theatre as complete neglect.

Information, please. "Do you have any good tickets left? Where are they? How much are they? Can you hear what they say from there? What's the name of the show? What's it about? What time does it start? What time does it let out? Is it really good?" These and countless related questions come over the telephone. The person who answers should know precisely what to say and how to say it. He or she must be alert, fully informed, and keenly interested in both the theatre and its patrons. The right person on the telephone can carry the theatre a long way; the wrong one can soon put it out of business. Fair or not, it is perfectly natural for people to judge the theatre by a single voice which represents it; any organization which meets the public such as a church, school, or business house is necessarily evaluated by its public representatives.

If the theatre is alert, it will put someone on the telephone who has the following qualifications: (1) a complete knowledge of the program in all its details, including dates, names of plays, authors, directors, seating plan, and parking facilities; (2) the qualities of good salesmanship, including the proper technique for opening and closing a sale; (3) a pleasant voice, clear articulation, good diction, and impeccable grammar. It is not likely that someone who has these qualifications will drop in and take over the job for the honor, but theatres that are doing a thriving business usually have such a qualified person. What often happens is that the assignment goes to someone who has nothing to do, or to someone who just loves to stand around the theatre waiting for a part in a play—someone who knows nothing of the responsibilities and who really did not want to do the work anyway. Such a person in the box office or on the telephone can drive away good prospects faster than the promotion department can bring them in. Insolence in any public office is unforgivable.

Radio Advertising

There is an old bit of homely advice which has not gone out of date:

> Remember well and bear in mind
> A good true friend is hard to find.
> And when you find one tried and true,
> Change not the old one for the new.

Has the glamour and glitter of television caused us to desert our old friend, radio, and somewhat prematurely? Radio has long been an important medium of show-business advertising, and the number of radio sets being sold every year is unbelievably high in spite of the popularity of television. The gains of television cannot be charged as losses to radio. Today practically every home has at least one radio set and many have two or three or more. A high percentage of automobiles have a radio as part of standard equipment. Thousands of little portables are carried to beaches, offices, games, and even to schools. In almost any gathering of a hundred or more one will find a portable radio and some ears glued to it. All citizens are advised by civil defense authorities to keep a battery radio in operating condition at all times. Radio has become an indispensable unit of our mass communication.

In theatre promotion radio can be used in a variety of ways, such as the following, for example:

1. Brief advertisements to be read by the station announcer.

2. Announcements of a few seconds each cut on records to be dubbed into various programs and inserted in the breaks.

3. Interviews with personalities of the show or with other personnel from the theatre, such as the director, the manager, or president of the theatre board.

4. Bits or short scenes from the shows themselves, which will arouse interest, yet not divulge so much of the play that people will feel that they know the play or can figure it out.

Brief advertisements to be read by the station announcer. Brief advertisements can merely be mailed to the stations. Ordinarily, but not always, the announcer will do a pretty fair job, especially if he is extended the courtesy of tickets to the show. It is better to send in fresh copy every day or two than to send a week's supply at one time. So much mail and so many requests go over the desk, that it is easy, sometimes even convenient, to lose everything but the work immediately at hand. These little advertisements may be only twenty, thirty, or sixty seconds long. Here is sample copy for a twenty-five-second announcement:

The big front curtain will rise on the opening production of the _____ Theatre next Thursday evening, January 17, at 8:30 P.M. The show will be *Witness for the Prosecution,* by Agatha Christie, which is described by New York critics as the "platinum-plated whodunit." Tickets for the production are now available at the central ticket office at _____. Prices range from $1.00 to $2.50. All seats are reserved and the sooner you come, the better your choice will be.

Educational and community theatres can often secure an amazing amount of advertising free or for a very small fee. Most such theatres can qualify as public-service organizations, and are therefore eligible for considerable free time, at least they should be able to purchase advertising for only a fraction of the cost—certainly they often receive many times the advertising they would be able to afford at commercial rates. It often happens that theatre and speech people are closely associated with radio stations of the community and will extend free time most graciously. Sometimes they will even make suggestions and give assistance. Big radio advertisers are often willing to allow some time on their own programs for such community ventures, providing, of course, that the advertising is in good taste and well prepared.

Brief announcement cut on records. Some radio stations prefer brief announcements or interviews cut on records. Three or four different thirty-second or one-minute interviews can be cut very inexpensively on a single record, the disc jockeys can fit them in when they need a little plug for the sake of variety. These usually receive considerable attention, since they require no effort on the part of the announcer and often give him a few seconds interval to adjust his work. Here is a sample of such a brief recorded interview (50 seconds):

ANNOUNCER: Here is a man with a word about a Broadway hit show that will be produced at the ⸺ Theatre next week. Mr. ⸺, what's new in theatre at your ⸺ theatre?

MR. ⸺: Next Tuesday, March 2, *The Country Girl* is coming to (this city).

ANNOUNCER: Is this a show you would call "rural" comedy?

MR. ⸺: It is a fiercely affectionate anecdote about theatre people. Its characterizations are rich and absorbing. Critics acclaimed it as one of the best plays of recent years. The story concerns a certain triangle and the rehabilitation of an alcoholic actor.

ANNOUNCER: Sounds very interesting. Anybody in it our listeners will know?

MR. ⸺: Yes, indeed! There is an excellent cast. The leading man is ⸺, a local favorite who has appeared in several very successful productions, and ⸺, who played in the productions of ⸺ and ⸺ last season. It is directed by ⸺.

ANNOUNCER: Ladies and gentlemen . . . make it a date to see *The Country Girl* beginning March 2nd and running through the 6th. ⸺ Theatre at ⸺. Tickets on sale at ⸺ and ⸺.

Radio stations are usually willing to give from one to fifteen-minute interviews on popular programs with artists, where they get right down and discuss values of the show and purposes of school and community theatre. The publicity man who takes a list of such possibilities to local stations will be delighted to see how pleasantly his ideas are received.

Longer interviews, or excerpts. Longer interviews may be live or recorded, depending upon circumstances. If a director is willing to do a lot of work and the station is willing to cooperate, a scene from the show may attract considerable attention. Stations like these scenes because they sound like drama rather than advertising. Of course, the commercial can be tacked on before and after the scene is played. A word of caution should be noted here: Unless these scenes are done well, with sufficient rehearsal, they may be worse than useless. People will say, "Well, that's something I don't want to see."

There are certain radio programs which have a definite relationship and a fitness to the theatre. If theatre inserts and postscripts can find their way into such broadcasts, so much the better; and obversely, other programs, such as sporting events, would be worth very little no matter how many times they come on.

In any event, consistent and repeated advertising in radio, as in any medium, is highly important for the best results.

Television Advertising

Theatre people are naturally concerned with what television will mean to them. Only time can give the complete answer. Many believe that this new medium will become the greatest source of entertainment in the history of the world. No one can doubt that it has made tremendous strides in recent years and that with improved programming, color screens, and over-all advances, progress will continue. It is almost impossible to believe that as late as 1945 there were only twenty-five thousand television sets in the United States. In 1960 there were 56 million sets, and, of course, audiences had increased proportionately. However, to correct any impression that radio is being sacrificed for television, it should be added that there has been a consistent yearly gain in the sale of radios; it is estimated that there are now over 156 million radio sets in America—about three to a family. Jack Benny says, "Dramatic programs have improved tremendously and eventually will be almost as exciting as an evening in the theatre. I say almost, because I don't think anything will ever replace the live theatre for drama and pure enjoyment. The theatre has survived the threat of silent and sound motion pictures and then radio—and will survive the threat of television."

Can television help the theatre? Yes, especially the noncommercial theatre, which can receive without cost some of the time set aside for public service. It can utilize such time to arouse interest in the living theatre. For example, it can present short dramatic scenes from shows that are to be fully staged in the theatre. If such teasers are well done, they provide excellent publicity.

A word of warning on the use of dramatic scenes from copyrighted plays is in order: Some authors and publishers will not permit any part of their plays to be used on television for the purpose of advertising, even though the theatre is paying royalty for its use on the stage; some specify the use of a certain number of lines; a few have little or no restriction. The proper and legal way to settle this question is to secure in advance written permission from the author or publisher—or sometimes both. Copyrighted material must be cleared for the protection of all concerned. There is, of course, no problem regarding the use of plays whose copyrights have run out. Plays, like books, may be copyrighted in the United States for twenty-eight years and renewed once for an additional twenty-eight years, making a total of fifty-six years; after that, a play automatically is in the public domain.

Spot announcements can also be worked in around the acts on television.

Most theatres simply could not afford to purchase advertising time at commercial rates. Their only hope lies in tactfully working with television and sharing talent but never fighting with the young and powerful big brother. If cooperation with television is not the key, probably one does not exist.

Photographs

Every division of show business, be it opera, concert, symphony, or theatre, depends to a considerable degree on photographs. The charm and power of an eye-catching picture is almost irresistible. It is not unheard of for people to look at a picture display and then go in and buy tickets without the slightest idea of what the show is about. Many professional companies have what they call a "frame" about 4×6 feet in the lobby, with a number of interesting photographs attractively arranged on it. For a hundred years the frame has been an indispensable part of show business. People stand around and look at it before, during, and after the show. Because show business is favored with beautiful women and handsome men, their pictures are given tremendous emphasis and attention. In Hollywood and New York, expert photographers specialize in show-business pictures. Such famous revues as Earl Carroll's *Vanities* and Ziegfield's *Follies* used the pictures of beautiful girls in every piece of advertising sent out. The selection of beauties ranged through sweet, demure, coy, innocent, languid, sexy, and sultry. The purpose is of course to make one want to see the show.

The use of photographs is one point of professional show business that the average amateur group should investigate. First of all, it is important to find a competent theatrical photographer. This might be accomplished by having a sort of photographers' contest on some play, letting each one choose some subjects and situations and show what he can do. A good photographer is not necessarily a good theatrical photographer. Such work requires a certain skill and imagination, a knowledge of how to focus attention, and to get from the actors the right motivation. Theatre pictures should have animation, conflict, or mystery. Too often a picture is taken with several people looking all around: one at the camera, one to the right, one to the left, and one merely grinning at the others. Another ineffective pose often seen is the family-album type, where everyone is lined up and looking straight ahead. Such a picture may be good for the records, but it is not of much value in selling the show. Why not consider love scenes, duels, intrigues, challenges, comic situations, or dramatic moments? Newspapers are just as anxious as theatrical promoters to have pictures that will capture attention; consequently many of them send their own photographers. Directors and designers often want pictures of the sets; they have put in so much work on them that they believe it only fair to show the pictures. Here one must forget about fairness and get on with selling the show. If such pictures are really interesting and will help sell the show, they might be used; otherwise, leave them out of promotion. They are excellent for teaching classes and for the study of scenic design, but one will have a hard time selling them to the public or the press.

The following bits of advice as to the kinds, preparation, and use of photographs are suggested by experienced show people:

1. Make the pictures glossy rather than soft or matte finish. Newspaper engravings cannot be made sharp and clear from soft finish.

2. Get at least five or six different poses to serve for the press and for posters.

3. Don't crowd too many faces on one picture unless there is some special reason. Three large faces are better than several small ones.

4. Use as many different poses and as many people as you can. The people playing minor parts are entitled to recognition also.

5. The most useful size is 8″ × 10″ or 10″ × 12″. Make enough prints to do the job well.

6. It is extremely important to have the cast well costumed, well made-up, and above all, in character. A hastily donned costume and poor make-up will give the production a bad press.

7. See to it that those photographed have a focal point of interest and that they are not merely gazing around.

8. Contrast in background is of paramount importance. Dark costumes should be taken against light background and light against dark. A man and woman wearing dark clothes in front of a black background may look acceptable on the set, but not on photograph.

9. The job of taking publicity pictures should be planned in advance and never hurried. Unless there is time enough to do it well, it may be worse than nothing. Pictures posed and taken in a hurry are apt to show poorly adjusted clothing, buttons undone, stray locks of hair, careless make-up, and inappropriate attitude.

10. When picture displays are used in a frame, the individual pictures should be in neat, glass-covered frames that are properly fastened by screws or bolts to the big frame. Usually small bolts are better than screws for the reason that they prevent the pictures from being stolen by pranksters or autograph collectors. Another often used frame is constructed with one large glass cover similar to a full glass door which serves as a close fitting overall cover to keep the pictures neatly in place. Individual pictures can be affixed to the background with thumb tacks, rubber cement, or tape. A lock for the frame is a good investment.

If the theatre has a choice place for picture display, it may be well worth the time and expense to prepare a frame with light behind it and have the pictures reproduced on colored transparency film such as ad-lux or translite. This is extra trouble, but it is a tremendous attention-getter.

FIG. 23.

This is an action picture of girls in ballet performance. The pictures are clear and the contrast is good.

FIG. 24.

This excellent picture of Coe Glade as Carmen portrays the mood and character of the famous gypsy.

FIG. 25.   This picture of Tossy Spivakovsky portrays animation in the finest sense.   It gives the impression of a real artist.

FIG. 26.

A lovely ballet dancer is photographed. This is an ideal way to take a
picture as she performs.

Announcements to Clubs, Classes, and Groups

A few years ago a western university decided to stage a different Shakespearean play each year, with an abridged version of an hour's length presented in matinees for the high school students in the area. The idea worked out rather well except in one large high school, where only twenty students signed up. Other high schools of similar size were sending several hundred. After three years of such discouraging results, the theatre manager went to the principal to see what could be done to stimulate greater interest. The principal received him graciously and said, "I'm very sorry. We had our teachers announce this fine play, but the students just aren't interested. We have done the best we can. Our students don't seem to want Shakespeare. Maybe next year they will be more interested." The theatre management felt sure that the lack of interest was due to the way it was announced. Accordingly, the next year they persuaded the high school principal to allow some university theatre students to visit all the English classes and present a five-minute announcement about *Antony and Cleopatra*. The students who carried out this assignment were well-dressed, well-rehearsed, and well-informed. When they entered the classrooms they were careful to show proper respect and courtesy to the teacher as well as to the students. Each announcer had some pictures of settings and actors to furnish a little background on the play. The result? Four hundred students came from the school to the first matinee—a 1,600 per cent gain. The only difference from other years was that the announcements were given by people who were well-prepared and enthusiastic. The high school principal seemed highly pleased, but merely said, "I guess the kids are more interested in Shakespeare than they used to be."

Anouncements before clubs and classes can be effective only if those doing the job are thoroughly prepared in all ways. This means getting the information, assimilating it well, and carefully rehearsing every word and movement from the time one enters the room until he leaves.

Contrary to common belief, it is not hard to get permission to give a five-minute announcement before almost any service organization or club. If the preparation is thorough, five minutes is long enough; if not, it is too long by five minutes. If the announcement is to be made before the Kiwanis Club, send a young woman to speak; if it is to be made before the League of Women Voters, send a young man. The messenger is as important as the message, maybe more so.

It is rather common to think of an announcement as some dull routine to which no one pays any attention. A good announcement should be a concise speech to persuade, not a speech merely to inform.

To begin the project, the management should secure a list of all civic clubs, parent-teachers associations, churches, and other local organizations from the Chamber of Commerce. Someone of maturity and prestige should then call or write the presidents of these groups and ask for the privilege of making an announcement on the desired date. If this date is not available ask for the next best opening.

Many people are too timid, too shy and sensitive to ask for this favor.

There are literally hundreds of spots that could be utilized to get in a good plug for the theatre, but it takes some exploration to find them and some work to carry on the campaign.

Miscellaneous Devices for Promotion

Many other excellent devices for promotion can be adapted to suit the personality of the theatre, being sure to keep well within the limits of good taste in whatever is done. If there is any group in the world that should be able to develop new and different ideas, the theatre is it. But so many people think only of acting in connection with the theatre. Those who might have excellent ideas for promotion do not always turn their talents in that direction.

Another success quality often lacking is courage. At a recent American Educational Theatre convention a national representative said, "We theatre people are too reticent and timid about going to school and community leaders and making our wants known. We need to tell our story with more confidence and aggressiveness."

Let there be contests of all kinds. (1) Queen contests are always in order; people and the press love them. You can get a front page picture of a queen in the paper more readily than you can a visiting scientist of national eminence. (2) Information contests by press, radio, and television are always in progress regardless of the scandals. For instance, when a Shakespeare play is presented the college paper can run a list of twenty questions about the play and the author and give a prize for the first complete set of answers. English students can prepare such questions. (3) An outline drawing of characters in the play can be published in the newspaper, with prizes offered for the best coloring job sent in. (4) Attendance contests between sororities and fraternities sometimes work well if there is some special incentive.

Desk and wall calendars are usually successful. Some of the leading college theatres in the nation, such as those at Oregon, Delaware, Minnesota, and Cornell, make regular use of them. Dates of theatre productions are usually set off in colored squares for emphasis. Everyone likes an attractive calendar. See the examples on page 117.

Bookmarks and blotters may be circulated through libraries most effectively. It is well to have a good friend in the library who will see to it that the supply is kept fresh and neat and that the janitor helps by not scooping everything into the wastebasket each night. Many janitors who can't tell a pile of dirt from a pile of snow just love to clean off bits of advertising and pull down posters. Don't scold them, convert them; they need friends too.

Dogs and other pets can sometimes help advertise. Hunter College once sent someone around with a beautiful dog and an announcement to hand out which said, "I'm Flush. I live at 50 Wimpole Street." The announcement went on to tell about the Barretts and Mr. Browning in a most intriguing way. It was a wonderful device for arousing interest in the show. This idea could no doubt be used in a number of plays. There is a lion in *Androcles and the Lion,* horses participate in *Oklahoma.*

Costume displays in downtown windows are helpful in advertising elaborate costume plays, of which there are many. Exhibits of what people wear to the opera or theatre make a natural combination.

An effective device that should not be overlooked is an inexpensive insert to be sent out by department stores with their regular bills. It might read somewhat as follows:

The _____ Store recommends the current production of the Civic Theatre, entitled _____, playing on November 7 through November 14. It is a delightful entertainment which the entire family can enjoy.

Even public utilities can often be persuaded to stamp a note on their billings, and these cover practically the entire city.

In some localities the ordinary little matchbooks provide effective theatre advertisements. Boldface type on smooth white stock can give the name, location, and telephone number of the theatre, as well as the titles and dates of the season of plays. Match books cost from a half cent to a cent each depending on the quantity purchased. Case lots or more (2,500 books), may be purchased for about $12.

Card 1 — University Theatre Calendar

HANG ◯ UP

UNIVERSITY THEATRE CALENDAR

1948 - 1949

NOVEMBER 1948
"Lady In The Dark"

S	M	T	W	T	F	S
	1	2	3	4	5	6
7	8	9	10	11	12	13
14	15	16	17	18	19	20
21	22	23	24	25	26	27
28	29	30				

DECEMBER 1948
"Dark Of The Moon"

S	M	T	W	T	F	S
			1	2	3	4
5	6	7	8	9	10	11
12	13	14	15	16	17	18
19	20	21	22	23	24	25
26	27	28	29	30	31	

JANUARY 1949

S	M	T	W	T	F	S
						1
2	3	4	5	6	7	8
9	10	11	12	13	14	15
16	17	18	19	20	21	22
23	24	25	26	27	28	29
30	31					

FEBRUARY 1949
"Petrified Forest"

S	M	T	W	T	F	S
		1	2	3	4	5
6	7	8	9	10	11	12
13	14	15	16	17	18	19
20	21	22	23	24	25	26
27	28					

MARCH 1949
"The Vigil"

S	M	T	W	T	F	S
		1	2	3	4	5
6	7	8	9	10	11	12
13	14	15	16	17	18	19
20	21	22	23	24	25	26
27	28	29	30	31		

APRIL 1949
"Othello"

S	M	T	W	T	F	S
					1	2
3	4	5	6	7	8	9
10	11	12	13	14	15	16
17	18	19	20	21	22	23
24	25	26	27	28	29	30

MAY 1949
"Spring Festival Play"

S	M	T	W	T	F	S
1	2	3	4	5	6	7
8	9	10	11	12	13	14
15	16	17	18	19	20	21
22	23	24	25	26	27	28
29	30	31				

JUNE 1949

S	M	T	W	T	F	S
			1	2	3	4
5	6	7	8	9	10	11
12	13	14	15	16	17	18
19	20	21	22	23	24	25
26	27	28	29	30		

1

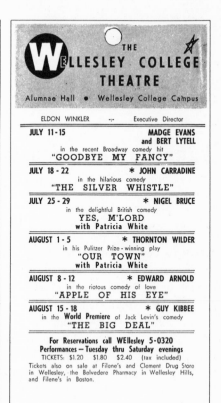

THE

WELLESLEY COLLEGE THEATRE

Alumnae Hall • Wellesley College Campus

ELDON WINKLER -:- Executive Director

JULY 11-15 **MADGE EVANS and BERT LYTELL**
in the recent Broadway comedy hit
"GOODBYE MY FANCY"

JULY 18 - 22 ✻ **JOHN CARRADINE**
in the hilarious comedy
"THE SILVER WHISTLE"

JULY 25 - 29 ✻ **NIGEL BRUCE**
in the delightful British comedy
YES, M'LORD
with Patricia White

AUGUST 1 - 5 ✻ **THORNTON WILDER**
in his Pulitzer Prize - winning play
"OUR TOWN"
with Patricia White

AUGUST 8 - 12 ✻ **EDWARD ARNOLD**
in the riotous comedy of love
"APPLE OF HIS EYE"

AUGUST 15 - 18 ✻ **GUY KIBBEE**
in the World Premiere of Jack Levin's comedy
"THE BIG DEAL"

For Reservations call WEllesley 5-0320
Performances — Tuesday thru Saturday evenings
TICKETS: $1.20 $1.80 $2.40 (tax included)
Tickets also on sale at Filene's and Clement Drug Store
in Wellesley, the Belvedere Pharmacy in Wellesley Hills,
and Filene's in Boston.

2

FIG. 27.

1. The calendar idea of announcing dates and plays first came to the authors attention in 1948. Since then many theatres have used it and say that it is effective. The idea of punching a hole at the top end which says "Hang Up" may keep the calendar on the wall all year.

2. The neat post card size gives considerable information in a condensed form. People will often hang up a small card for handy reference whereas they would not use something large.

X

PREPARATION OF THE PRINTED PROGRAM

The variety of the printed theatre programs from many schools and theatres reveals an infinitely wide range of conditions, regulations, and tastes. It is possible to find everything from a simple mimeographed sheet to an elaborate booklet with a four-color cover. Programs may be large or small, narrow or wide, simple or complex, conservative or ultra, comprehensive or limited.

Despite the variety, there are guideposts and precautions which should be neither overlooked nor bypassed. For instance, all programs should carry the name of the theatre, producing organization, show dates, and the name of the city and state. Unfortunately, the year is often omitted on the program, making it impossible to check for theatre history. An outsider examining a program should be able to find out what, when, where and by whom a play is presented.

Values of the Program or Playbill

A distinctive and well-planned playbill, of which the organization can be proud, has multiple functions including the following:

1. A source of advertising revenue and a link with business firms.

2. A direct medium for acquainting the public with the theatre's place in community life, its purposes, and its policies.

3. Detailed information concerning the schedule of plays, dates, try-outs, parking facilities, refreshments, rest rooms, etc.

4. An official announcement of the theatre board of directors, cast, author, director, manager, technical director, stagehands, designers, costumers, make-up artists, understudies, and other personnel.

5. Notes about the play, synopsis of scenes, and who's who in the cast.

6. Courtesies such as patron lists, acknowledgments for stage furnishings and other special services to the theatre.

7. Publicity for the theatre (both local and national).

Cover Design and Colors

An appropriate cover design will set the mood and add interest to the play. This does not necessarily mean an elaborate or detailed design, for there are many ways to adapt a cover to a title with dignity and charm. Simplicity can often enhance the relationship between the program and the play. If your front cover is overcrowded you lose the dignity and simplicity which are so important. An overcrowded cover is like an overcrowded display window; the effect is one of cheapness and the result is loss of interest.

The selection of colors is likewise important to the printed program. The symbolism of color has long been known for its dramatic power.

Preparation of the Copy

Errors in the printed program, whether they be sins of omission or of commission, can bring misery to the theatre. All too often in the rush of preparing the play, the printed program is given hurried, shabby treatment. Yet if names are omitted, misspelled, or wrongly placed, someone is likely to be hurt or offended. Sometimes an error, such as the interchange of names and placement of wrong ones under pictures, has made it necessary to throw away an entire printed order. In rare cases even lawsuits have resulted. A mistake in print, however small, is permanent. Errors in printing names and titles will be neither forgotten nor forgiven. Some of the bitterest fights in show business concern the billing of artists.

Neat typewritten copy and well-laid-out dummy with appropriate markings indicating type sizes and placement will reduce costs and facilitate printing. It is expensive and highly unsatisfactory to pay a typesetter to decipher copy, and it is a legitimate expense for a printer to charge extra for corrections and additions on the proof which were no fault of his.

Before a program goes to press those responsible for it should sit down and go over every item for spelling, placement, titles, arrangement, and pagination with meticulous care. Errors get by even the best proofreaders. Inexperienced ones do not understand how important and how difficult the assignment is. It is a good idea for two people to check the copy as they read it aloud word for word. The program is no place for speed reading.

Advertising in the Printed Program

An attractive program adorned with paid advertisements will usually increase public interest and create a better feeling of unity among all concerned.

Program advertising can not only pay off all costs of its printing, but also make money if properly handled. Many advertisers will buy your space if the idea is presented on a business basis. Why not sell it to them?

When you meet prospective buyers, don't act as if you were soliciting contributions or begging for charity. *Sell* the advertising! The program salesman who says, "You ought to support the theatre and buy this advertisement!" should lose the sale—and he probably will. Prejudice against this advertising medium will fade away when you make it worth something, get the right kind of display copy, and the proper support from the theatre. Once you establish the idea that your program space has value on a par with other media, you will have little difficulty selling it. If the copy has the right appeal it will fulfill its purpose and please the advertiser.

Selling advertising requires consistent work, careful planning, and keen imagination. It is not a hit-and-miss business, but must be built up over a period of years. The alert salesman will suggest the right association of the advertisement to the theatre. For example, one photographer was sold the idea of inserting a half-page advertisement featuring an attractive portrait by him of the leading lady of the current play. Everyone commented about it as a most clever feature. In fact, the advertising proved so successful that the photographer bought the space permanently. A costume company highlighted a half-page display with pictures of well-known local actors wearing the company's fabrics. Everyone read the advertisement and the tie-in was perfect. Through playbills, restaurants and cafés often cater to after-the-show theatre parties; displays of ready-to-wear apparel and hair stylings have a special appropriateness for theatre programs. Taxicabs are a natural for theatregoers.

In many cities there are advertising agencies which are in search of appropriate media for their clients. Get acquainted with these agencies, explain the values of your program, and get their suggestions.

The chief appeal from the buyer's point of view is price. Prices for space should be realistically evaluated, with a strong incentive for buying the larger spaces. For example, if a whole page sells for $50, the half-page should be $30, or more than half the price of the full page; one-fourth page should be $20, or more than half the price of the half-page.

The most important factor in selling an ad is the salesman himself. He should be well supplied with attractive samples and compelling suggestions. He should be enthusiastic, well-prepared, and possess a high degree of initiative and resourcefulness. He should believe wholeheartedly in his product and work persistently toward increasing the value of his advertising medium.

A successful advertisement is the direct result of cooperation between the one who sells and the one who buys.

> He who has a thing to sell
> And goes and whispers down the well;
> Is not so apt to get the dollars
> As he who climbs a tree and hollers.

Selection of Paper

About one-third of the price of the printed program goes for paper, providing there is minimum waste. If there is excess or more than medium waste, paper will account for an even higher part of the total cost. The selection of standard or most economical sizes is therefore highly important. Off-standard sizes can hardly be justified; if an off-size is selected, the price will go up sharply. Make the job fit the paper, not the paper the job. That makes for efficient production in a great majority of printed pieces.

Printers purchase paper from supply houses in five standard or basic sizes, from which any of the following program page sizes can be cut without waste: $4\frac{1}{2}'' \times 6''$, $5'' \times 8''$, $5\frac{1}{2}'' \times 8\frac{1}{2}''$, $6'' \times 9''$, $8'' \times 10''$, $8\frac{1}{2}'' \times 11''$, $9'' \times 12''$. Most printers recommend for programs a "book paper" from 50- to 70-pound weight. (This weight refers to what 500 sheets of paper, size $25'' \times 38''$, will weigh.) Programs can, of course, be made from other types of paper, such as bond, cover, poster, or even cheaper news print.

Choosing the right make and grade of paper is a technical problem that is best done by the printer, because he usually knows more about paper, knows the market, and knows exactly what is wanted. Once a printer knows the nature of your needs he will be your best adviser. Before a program is begun, it is advisable to visit your printer to look at samples and get suggestions and prices. Advance planning is highly desirable.

Printers' Types

Type faces are like human faces—each has its own expression. Through the medium of type and its multitude of designs, salient points can be expressed forcefully and convincingly. No matter what typographic effect you desire, you can achieve it by studying the selection of type faces available at any good printing shop. Because it is not feasible for printers to carry a large variety of type faces, each printer selects a few which he believes most suitable. He usually has these available in a full range of sizes.

Anyone who has anything to do with printing should know a few important fundamentals about typography. Selection of appropriate styles, sizes, and arrangement is vitally important to the printed word. Because most theatres are dimly lighted, it is of utmost importance that the type of the theatre program be clear and easily read. Small, ornate, and crowded typography will be of little or no value to the customers.

In a rather general way, types are divided into five basic groups— roman, italic, gothic (or sans-serif), script, and text—plus various special- effect types. Variations of these are developed under such names as Bodoni, Cairo, Caslon, Century, Cheltenham, Futura, Gallia, Garamond, Goudy, Karnak, and others. Actually there are 1,475 different type faces in the United States today, and each of these faces is designed in upper case, lower case, italics, light face, boldface, etc. If one multiplies all this by all the sizes ranging from 6-point to 72-point, you can see that any comprehensive study would be a career in itself. But the size of the field need not keep one from knowing a few fundamentals.

Type is usually measured in points and picas. There are 72 points to the inch, or 6 picas. A pica is 12 points. Most newspapers are printed in 8-point type. The text of a theatre program is generally set in 10- or 12-point. A 6-point size is too small for most purposes, though it might be used if there were some reason to micrify a feature of the program. This is little better than complete omission, but it does give formal recognition in limited space. Many types that are not intended for large lettering come in sizes ranging from 6 to 36 points. Title covers on theatre programs usually range from 24 to 48 points in size. Occasionally, some are 72 points (one inch).

Several other matters of composition will add interest and variety besides the selection of type: short paragraphs, plenty of white space, alternate light and boldface paragraphs, conversational subheads, and large initials for each paragraph—these give life to the page. An endless variety of effects can be obtained from selection and arrangement of type.

Many printing shops have type-specimen books available which give style and size as well as suggestions for good usage. An hour or two spent at the printer's can be invaluable for gaining the necessary knowledge. If he knows that you are interested and particular about selection of type and composition, he will be more likely to see that your work is well done. Figures 28–29.

Final Proofreading

The last chance to overtake an error in the printed program is with the proofreader. If he misses it, it will be printed. Because there are so many kinds of errors and so many ways of making them, proofreaders never become overconfident. Let anyone who thinks proofreading is easy check the copy of the following three titles of plays:

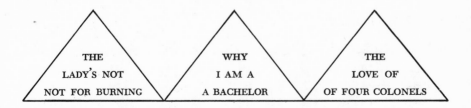

There is an error in each triangle, but it is hard to pick out. If you will read *aloud, word for word,* you will find the error. These triangles are tricky, but no trickier than much of the proof which must be read. If you omit the comma from the sentence, "Let's eat, mother," you have an error that only the most ungrateful cannibal would utter. First of all, the proofreader must understand the text of what he is reading; second, he must be sharp on grammar, punctuation, and spelling. What often happens is that some big error will go bowling through while the search for the little ones is on.

24-Point Caslon Bold

The newspaper is your

30-Point Stellar Bold

The newspaper is your basic

36-Point Tempo Black

The newspaper

42-Point Stygian Italic

The newspaper is

60-Point Coronet

The newspaper is yo

72-Point Cameo

ABCD

84-Point Condensed Gothic—Caps Only

ABCDEFG

FIG. 28.

Every advertiser should know something about type faces and sizes. A study of the foregoing types will be helpful. A little study in the selection of type will pay dividends.

PROOFREADERS MARKS

Symbol	Meaning	Symbol	Meaning
_e_ OR _S_	DELETE. TAKE OUT LETTERS OR WORDS INDICATED	Λ >	CARET. INSERT AT THIS POINT ADDITIONS (IN MARGIN)
_S_	DELETE AND CLOSE UP	⌢	INSERT COMMA HERE
OR #2	CLOSE UP, NO SPACE	V̇	INSERT APOSTROPHE
#	INSERT SPACE	V"	DOUBLE QUOTES
V⌒	LESS SPACE	⊙	INSERT PERIOD
VΛ	EVEN SPACE	⊙	" COLON
⌣	LOWER LETTER OR WORD	?|	" QUESTION MARK
⌢	ELEVATE "	9	TURN INVERTED LETTER
[	MOVE TO LEFT	X	REPLACE IMPERFECT TYPE
]	" TO RIGHT	A̲	REPLACE INDICATED LETTER WITH CAPITAL
=	STRAIGHTEN LINE	A̸	REPLACE WITH LOWER CASE
\\	ALIGN TYPE	wf	TYPE FACE WRONG FONT
ld>	INSERT LEAD BET. LINES	stet	LET IT STAND AS IS
□	INDENT (ONE EM)	(sp)	SPELL OUT
¶	MAKE NEW PARAGRAPH	caps	SET IN CAPITAL LETTERS
no ¶	RUN IN SAME "	sc	" " SMALL CAPS.
tr. OR ⌣	TRANSPOSE	lc	LOWER CASE LETTERS
(?)	QUERY (SEE MARGIN)	ulc	UPPER AND LOWER CASE

ital · _Italic_ · _rom_ · (Roman) · **bf** · **Bold Face** · CAPITALS · SMALL CAPITALS

(NOTE USE OF UNDERLINES)

FIG. 29.

Proofreading should include checking proof against the copy, seeing that all previous corrections are inserted, rechecking names and titles, and finally, faithfully using the dictionary.

Proof of advertising copy must also be scrutinized. If possible, the advertiser should see and approve *in writing* the copy which will run. If it is not possible for him to read his final copy, you must give it special care with copy in hand. An error in advertising can easily prevent your collecting for the space. Such things as wrong price listing or misspelling an adjective may mean that you cannot even distribute the programs—you dare not. For example, because the single letter *t* was left out of the word, *immortals,* no programs were distributed for one play, because the error made the message read, "Steinway Piano, Instrument of the Immorals." It's fun to laugh at the proof errors of others, but when it happens to us the humor fades.

The Finished Program

An attractive playbill packed with interesting information about the show will be prized and kept as a souvenir; the cheap, meager sheet will be thrown on the floor to be swept up by the janitor. The public will have the same regard for your program that you do.

Every effort should be made to have printed programs ready a few days before the show opens. There are several advantages: Your newspaper critics will appreciate the orientation of an advance copy, especially if the deadline is close. The cast will be delighted with a preview of the program. Printed programs posted at the box office before the show will stimulate public interest.

It is good business and good public relations to mail programs promptly to your advertisers, to other theatres, and to leading supporters of the theatre just before or at the same time the curtain rises. Everyone likes to have a program or a newspaper that is up to the minute; on the contrary, no one cares much about what is out of date. Public interest is ephemeral. Occasionally—perish the thought—your patrons will cling to the playbill as the only real evidence they possess of an evening in the theatre.

How many programs should you print? Experience shows that you will need two printed programs for every three members of the audience. It is the custom to give one program to a couple, but sometimes patrons will ask for an extra copy; and you will, of course, need one program for each customer who comes alone. Count in also those mentioned above. It averages out that you'll need about one thousand programs for fifteen hundred people. To print more than necessary is a waste, but it is better to have too many than too few. Your estimate should be realistic.

When a pleasant, enthusiastic usher hands the customer a program, it marks the beginning of an enjoyable evening. It sets the mood and makes a favorable impression.

PART TWO

During the Show

XI

HOW TO MEET, GREET, AND TREAT THE PUBLIC

Is there any specific rule for dealing with the public? There is—the Golden Rule; and almost everyone for the past two thousand years has heard of it. Here is precisely what it says: "Therefore all things whatsoever ye would that men should do to you, do ye even so to them: for this is the law and the prophets" (Matt. 7:12). Mark the last seven words, ". . . this is the law and the prophets." That's it. How simple! We ought to try it, especially in theatre business where so many of our problems are human ones. Someone has said, "Christianity hasn't failed; it just hasn't been tried." Maybe that is what is wrong with the Golden Rule—it presents a formula which has not really been tried. Incidentally, this rule is very similar to Immanuel Kant's famous categorical imperative: "Act only on that maxim whereby thou canst at the same time will that it should become a universal law." Which author is more readily understood?

Many successful men have adopted the Golden Rule as a business fundamental. For instance, Alfred C. Fuller said, "I learned early that if you have a good product and are polite to people, they will be polite to you." And who was Alfred C. Fuller? Well, last year his firm grossed nearly a hundred million dollars on brushes.

How to meet, greet, and treat the public might be answered by asking in all sincerity and candor, "How would we like to be treated if we were the theatre customers?" Would it not be a good idea to start with a customer and follow him through an evening of the theatre from the time he leaves his home until he returns? For the sake of completeness, lets assume that we are dealing with a new citizen of the community who does not even know where the theatre is. To get there he will need some sort of directions—an "arrivalogue." For example:

From the large fountain in the center of town go south two blocks to Second Street, which is also Highway 30. Turn right (west) and proceed for seven blocks to Grand Street where you again turn right. Here there is a large supermarket on the righthand corner where you turn. The theatre is less than a block from this corner and is on your right. There is a sign, "Civic Theatre," with an arrow below it pointing to the parking lot. An attendant will show you where to park.

One word of caution: avoid using the phrase, "You can't miss it." This may be embarrassing. It is true that you cannot give everyone an arrivalogue from his own home, but with directions from well-known landmarks, people can figure things out pretty well.

Because the attendant on the parking lot is often the first employee the customer meets, it is important that he get things off to a good start. An expert in the carparking business suggests this procedure for attendants: "Before you attempt to direct the customer, give him a pleasant greeting. Step up briskly with a smile and a word of welcome—then discuss parking." If the customer has a pleasant impression on his first visit, it will put him in a good mood for the next contact; but if he gets off to a bad start with an unpleasant experience, he will be all set for a round with the next person he meets and will probably be reciting a soliloquy which closes with the refrain, "This is the last time I'll come to this lousy place, etc."

Just what are the qualifications of a parking attendant? He should wear a uniform. He should be alert and courteous at all times, even if people do not seem to appreciate his kindness. He should be able to give directions with clarity in a few words. He should be able to communicate with his hands and with flashlight signals which people can understand. And he most certainly should not shine the light in people's faces, as is often done. If he can do these few things when they should be done, he won't have to come on the double yelling, "Hey, buddy, don't park there; that's reserved for special guests." People know that such things are done, but they don't want to hear about them. It is much better to say, "This way, please—right in here; good. Thank you."

No tips for the parking attendant, ever. If he accepts such, people will soon believe that special privileges go along with the tips. Of course, the parking attendant should be paid adequately and he should take pride in the service. He should let the patrons know that parking is part of the theatre service.

For the convenience and protection of the customers, parking should be arranged systematically in rows of two so that one car is directly behind the other. There should be sufficient space so that the front car can drive forward, swing, and exit; the rear one can back out and exit. With such an arrangement, the customers can park their own cars and keep their keys. The fact that the attendant does not handle the steering wheels places the responsibility squarely with the patron, except for negligence, such as improperly marked parking lanes or poor directions. Ordinarily, minor problems of bent fenders due to driving are not the responsibility of the theatre, but such cases should be reported to the manager. In one case an attendant urged a driver, "Drive your car right up against the other." She did so and smashed out a tail light. In this case the theatre shared in the blame. It would have been better to say, "Drive your car within a foot or so," or "Drive up close to the car in front." There is a technical difference which any judge would be quick to notice.

In summary, it is quicker, safer and more satisfactory to let the customer handle his own car in so far as possible.

When the customer arrives in the lobby and walks over to the box office, the ticket seller will extend a pleasant "Good evening" or other appropriate greeting and then proceed with the "How many, please?" routine. At the close of the transaction, the ticket seller should give his or her best "Thank you." This "thank you" should be a special one because this is the place where the customer parts with his money. Even if the box office is rushed, there is still time for an appropriate "Thank you." Don't be curt, be courteous.

Everywhere, but particularly on Broadway, there has been so much criticism of box office rudeness that it may be well to look at some of the ways in which these two words "thank you" are expressed. We know that they must be spoken with the right attitude and feeling if they are to convey the right meaning. It is almost impossible to say a kind word with a bitter heart.

"Thank you" may have many shades of meaning, ranging from irony or even sarcasm to sincere graciousness, and the human ear can interpret them all for what they are.

The next contact our customer makes is with the ticket taker or door-man. This employee should tear off the seat stubs from the ticket and hand them to the customer with appropriate directions, such as "To your right, please." These words should wear a smile and be clear and pleasant. The magic of "please" and "thank you" is by no means a new discovery. An old anonymous aphorism evaluates it in these words:

> Hearts like doors, open with ease
> To very, very little keys.
> Don't forget there are two of these:
> "I thank you, sir" and "If you please."

In larger theatres there are often attendants who direct the crowds to more specific locations for better crowd management. Often beautiful girls in formal attire take care of these assignments. One of the smartest theatres on the Pacific Coast places a platinum blonde at each end of the lobby and a brunette in the center. The three lovely girls not only help direct traffic but also give the theatre a nice touch of style and attractive-ness. Comments on the idea have been most favorable.

It often happens that in smaller theatres the manager or other officer of the theatre knows nearly all the customers by name and would be able to recognize a stranger and extend to him a cordial greeting which would be appreciated. Moreover, such strangers are likely to tell their friends about the place where they were greeted so pleasantly. The New Testament recommends this technique in the following words (Heb. 13: 1–2):

1. Let brotherly love continue.
2. Be not forgetful to entertain strangers: for thereby some have entertained angels unawares.

Though the word "angels" has a slightly different meaning in the scriptures than it does in the theatre today, the reward is similar.

When our customer is escorted to his seat and presented with a printed program by a courteous usher, he will have made contacts with at least five people: (1) the parking lot attendant, (2) the ticket seller, (3) the doorman, (4) an official of the theatre, perhaps the manager or director of public relations, and (5) the usher. If all of them have been as alert and as courteous as they should have been, he will be in a good mood to see and appreciate the show. If a similar attitude is multiplied by the number in the audience, conditions are far above average. Courtesy is contagious, but some people don't catch it as easily as others do.

Our customer sees by the program that there are two intermissions, the first one fifteen minutes long and the second one ten minutes: so he strolls out to look around. He observes that the building is immaculate and attractively decorated, that the rest rooms are absolutely clean and sanitary. These things are important. He goes over to the refreshment stand, and to his surprise there is sufficient help to serve the people in the allotted time. Everyone is enjoying himself as if he were part of the show itself. Emily Dickinson wrote, "The show is not the show, but they that go." An audience is a beautiful feature of the theatre; those who attend should enjoy themselves and should certainly enjoy each other. This social aspect is an important part of every evening which cannot be duplicated and without which the event may be quite ordinary.

When our customer is back in his seat, ready for the next act, he senses that the temperature is neither too hot nor too cold. "These people know the difference between ventilation and refrigeration," he says to himself, as if this were not a common fact. Good acoustics, without which there is no satisfaction in theatregoing, has not been left to chance in the successful theatre. It is better if the acoustics are such that microphones are not needed, but if they are, they should be installed and used properly. In this day, when so much is known about the science of acoustics and loud-speakers, there is no point in asking people to strain their ears— even if they were willing to. But whether or not there are microphones, actors must be taught the importance of clear enunciation and articulation. If a sound is garbled when it is picked up, it comes out even worse, because all that is added is greater amplitude or loudness.

Somehow during the evening our new customer has lost his keys and does not miss them until the show is over. This could spoil the evening, but he has noticed on the printed program a little statement of policy regarding lost and found articles: "If you find a lost article, please bring it to the office; if you lose an article, please inquire at the office. If we have it, we will be pleased to return it." He goes to the office and the keys are there. Of course, he is pleased and says: "Could I leave a little reward for the finder?" The manager replies: "No indeed, we are happy to return them—one of the employees picked them up after intermission." Then he explains that the theatre receives a number of lost articles, such as gloves (especially single gloves), single earrings, keys, and wallets.

If a lost article is not turned in on the evening it is lost, the loser leaves his address and telephone number so that he may be informed as to whether or not the article is found.

When the show is over, the patrons should not be hurried out into the street as if there were some special need to evacuate the place immediately. Too often the customers are made to feel that there is some great urgency to get the lights turned out. There should be a graciousness about dismissing people; anyway, they can't all drive off the parking lot simultaneously. Our guest observes that in this case there is no rush or pressure about the whole evening. As he drives home, he is pretty sure to feel that the evening has been well spent and that this theatre is probably filling a need as a cultural community activity.

Keeping the old, faithful customer contented and happy should never be taken for granted, but it often is. Once you lose him, your chances for getting him back may be slim, even though he loves your theatre. One unfriendly act or slight may serve to break a line of devotion that has endured for years.

The old friend will want some variety in his play-going diet if his interest is to be continued. The same entertainment, like the same food, can get terribly monotonous. Once upon a time an old customer with a look of boredom on his face handed a manager a note as he left the theatre. On it was this biblical reference: "See Hebrews 13:8." When the manager got home he took down his dusty Bible and found the place: "Jesus Christ the same yesterday, and today, and for ever."

All over America theatre ventures ranging in cost from a few hundred dollars to many thousands have come and gone. The majority of them fail for lack of public support; only a few really succeed. Why did the theatre in X City succeed while the one in Z City folded? Did not Z City have a good program, competent actors, and capable director? Did not the people appreciate good theatre? Why didn't they support it? Sometimes we blame everything but the reason. Have we overlooked a public relations angle which, though very small, is always extremely vital?

Kindness is the key word in all successful public relations. For thousands of years its rewards have been extolled in songs, stories, and poems. Such universal favorites as *Androcles and the Lion, The Vision of Sir Launfal,* and *Abou Ben Adhem* approach the idea positively, while negative aspects are shown in such works as *The Rhyme of the Ancient Mariner, The Old Settlers Story,* and *King Lear.*

Few things distress a manager more than to have one of his employees treat a customer unkindly. The personal consideration of customers is just as important in the theatre as it is in any other business. The little poem by John B. O'Reilly, *What is Good,* should be part of the philosophy of every theatre:

> "What is the real good?"
> I asked in musing mood.
>
> Order, said the law court;
> Knowledge, said the school;
> Truth, said the wise man;
> Pleasure, said the fool;
> Love, said the maiden;
> Beauty, said the page;
> Freedom, said the dreamer;
> Home, said the sage;
> Fame, said the soldier;
> Equity, the seer;—
>
> Spake my heart full sadly,
> "The answer is not here."
>
> Then within my bosom
> Softly this I heard;
> "Each heart holds the secret;
> Kindness is the word."

One can go around and around the problem of how to meet, greet, and treat the public, but eventually, he will get back to the rule of "This is the law and the prophets."

XII

HOW TO UTILIZE REVIEWS AND PUBLIC OPINION

Public opinion and the reviews of radio, television, and newspaper critics can be made to serve theatre promotion and publicity effectively in two ways: (1) for immediate use while a play is actually in production, and (2) for promoting and selling the next season of plays.

Promoting a Current Production

With few exceptions, theatres everywhere have complained that after the review of the first night's performance the free publicity suddenly falls off especially in the press. Sometimes scarcely another word is printed after the reviews. It is not that radio, television, and the press dislike the shows; they merely feel that since the show is on its way, everything newsworthy has been said, and if the production needs further publicity it should buy it at advertising rates. So, unless the theatre publicity workers can come up with something new and interesting, there will be no more free space; the play is on its own.

Of course, it helps if the first-night audience is really wild about the show and calls up their friends to say: "Listen, don't you dare miss this play; it's the most wonderful entertainment we've seen in years." And if, in addition, the critics review it with estatic praise so that the whole town is talking, there might be enough momentum to carry it gloriously through the last performance. But the combination of such stimulating reactions is rare. Hits which bring spontaneous raves are the exception. They often catch the critics' fancy because of some timely aspect or some actor's special talent. What is more likely to happen is that the opening night will draw a small house and the advance publicity will be "too little and too late." Even with moderately enthusiastic reviews and a good audience, there must be extra publicity to catch and build the public interest. Well, what can the theatre do?

Make immediate, full, and complete use of favorable opinions and reviews. This has often been done successfully in a matter of hours. All radio and television stations should be alerted to the fact that they will receive highlights of the reviews and public opinion for early morning use with the newscasts. They will be told that such a report will be on disks or tape for them in ample time. This will mean some fast preparation by the theatre people, for they must strike while the iron is hot. It is the freshness that carries the appeal.

After a performance the audience enthusiasm is at its height, and it is easy to find customers who are willing to record some of this enthusiasm if it does not take too long. For this purpose it will be necessary to have a portable recorder and microphone conveniently located so that selected commentators from the audience can be invited to step over to the microphone and express their opinions of the play before they leave the theatre. It may even be wise to plan this some time between acts with the patrons whom you expect to participate. This will insure more interesting comments. After a number of responses have been recorded, it is a simple matter to select those which best serve the purpose.

The procedure might be something like the following:

ANNOUNCER: There must have been a most exciting performance at the theatre last night, judging from the applause and comments of the first-night audience which turned out to see William Shakespeare's comedy *A Midsummer Night's Dream* [or whatever the show was]. We take you to the theatre at the close of the show.

BEGIN
TRANSCRIPTION: (*Applause is on the record for a few seconds*).

MAN'S VOICE: It's been a wonderful evening. I didn't know that Shakespeare could be so much fun; I never laughed so hard in my life. This is one play that I can recommend for everyone.

WOMAN'S VOICE: I agree; it's just about the funniest show I ever saw. I don't know anything about Shakespeare, but

> (*laughing*) for anyone who wants humor, this is it.
> (*Other comments follow.*)
>
> THEATRE MANAGER: Plan to join us tonight or tomorrow night and enjoy *A Midsummer Night's Dream*. It's the hit of the season. Tickets are on sale all day every day at Sharp's Bookstore. Prices range from $.75 to $2.00. Join the fun.

Another way of getting the "come quick and see" comments before the public is to use selected quotations from newspaper reviews in the advertisements. These brief comments should be set in italics. Such choice bits as "Players sparkle in opening performance" and "First-nighters held spellbound by tense mystery" could be used. Television and radio can also make effective use of press comments.

When Charles Laughton and Paul Gregory opened a road show in Santa Barbara which drew an unusually rave review from an eminent critic, Producer Gregory made photostat copies of the review as soon as it rolled off the press and dispatched them by air mail to every theatre manager across the country where the show would appear on tour. Gregory's "quick-on-the-draw" technique was as impressive as the sensational story itself. He probably worked half the night getting everything ready, but it paid off handsomely.

Another excellent idea for immediate use is to have some well-known speech or English teacher go on the air with an interesting discussion of the author and his play. This may be a straight talk, or it could take the form of a discussion with others participating. Obviously the speaker should build up interest in the current production. In every community there are people who are competent to discuss a noted playwright and his work. Such discussion will make the play more worthwhile and enjoyable for the audience. There should be some plan of promotion for every single day throughout the run of the play so as to keep the event constantly before the public. "That which gets attention determines action" is an incontrovertible law of psychology.

During the time a show is in full swing is the ideal opportunity for letters to the editor. Such letters are sometimes referred to as "The Public Forum" or "What Our Readers Think." Practically every newspaper runs such a feature and all papers report that these letters are widely read. Letters about the play should be sent to this department or to the editor.

They should be short and to the point. If a number of people send them in, the results will be simply amazing. Sometimes a letter is contagious and will trigger a whole series if it happens to touch the hearts of the people. Often it is difficult to get people who plan to write to get their letters in the mail. Most of us are lazy and would rather talk about doing something than take action. We need encouragement and motivation before we act on even a good intention.

If a theatre has a telephoning committee, it has an excellent opportunity during the show. If the theatre does not have such a committee one should be promptly activated. Alert management will know on whom to depend to get such things done promptly. There are some people who enjoy telephoning but who would not write letters. Some will write letters rather than use the telephone. A little investigation and research will find the people who fit the assignments. The one thing to remember is that whatever is done must be done promptly if it is to be of value. It is not a problem for a committee to debate.

Promoting Future Productions

During the entire year the promotion department should be on the alert for reviews and public opinion which can be sifted over for the next season's campaign. These should include choice bits about the value of the theatre to the community, to education, and to entertainment. Enthusiastic comments of some visiting celebrity have great appeal. An opinion from an eminent visitor will be accepted as the purest evidence.

Just before the last act of the last play of the season, some well-liked theatre official should go before the audience with a thoroughly-prepared sales talk for the coming season. Members of the audience will have been supplied with order blanks in their programs and pencils will be furnished. The speech must be persuasive and brief, but not too brief to include the needful details and the proper dressing. It should include the promise of choice seats for the next season, discounts (if such are offered), and any special incentives to get prompt action. If this speech is done well it will be a tremendous boon. The late Margo Jones, well remembered for her success with the Dallas Theatre, was categorically opposed to going before an audience with a speech, but made a one-time exception to the rule for the purpose of selling the next season of plays. She did this before the beginning of the last act of the old season. After all, if the theatre fails to reclaim its patrons at the right moment, some other entertainment may grab them up during vacation. Another danger is that enthusiasm may wane when the patron gets away from the charm of the theatre. There is no point in waiting. If people want the entertainment, sign them up—the sooner the better. In the duet of "One Enchanted Evening," from *South Pacific*, the lovers alternately sing to each other: *"When you* find him (her) never let him (her) go." That is good show business. If it seems a bit on the high pressure side, just remember that there are many, some of whom are no longer in business, who ruefully wish they had not been so coy.

Some theatres like the idea of conducting an audience survey which will give all the patrons an opportunity to express preference, recommend changes, rate the plays, suggest new plays, comment on policy, and present new ideas. A gentle word of warning should be added at this point: It is best to make up the survey form so as to feature constructive and positive comments; play down the negative aspects. Once a well-known theatre director thought that the survey idea should be used as a fine, democratic method of letting the audience have a voice. But this particular survey seemed to call forth all gripes and complaints. The suggestions made were largely impracticable and useless. After the results were tabulated, the theatre director filed the report quietly away. No one on that staff has ever discussed it or suggested taking another. In all fairness to the idea, however, it should be known that other theatres have made excellent use of public opinion surveys and conduct them regularly.

The publication, *Critics' Reviews*, a collection of reviews of the New York leading newspapers covering the first performance of a new Broadway show, offers a tremendous wealth of commentary concerning the quality, nature, and theme of the play. Such a source of information is extremely helpful in preparing advertising and stories of all kinds. The comments and evaluations of recognized critics carry a high priority—some believe it is too high. A favorable comment from such a person as Brooks Atkinson may be extremely valuable and time saving.

Selected pictures from the current year or even from former years may be made into an effective montage. Such pictures must be chosen with care, for if they bring back memories of a play that was not well liked, or liked by only a few, the general effect may not be good. It certainly will not help to sell a show if a customer can put his finger on a picture and say, "Gee, I'll never forget that stinker." But if the pictures bring back pleasant memories and a touch of nostalgia, they will be worth the trouble. Well arranged pictures in the lobby often create considerable interest.

Professional people in show business often collect headlines of newspapers and compile them on a montage. The cumulative effect is impressive. These show the names of the newspapers, the headlines, and a little of the reading matter. Close inspection will show that none of the copy is derogatory. Best foot forward is the rule.

XIII

IT'S THE LAW

One of the most damaging things that can happen to a theatre is involvement in a lawsuit. It is even worse if the lawsuit involves a situation that could have been avoided or prevented. The study of prevention of legal troubles is just as important to business health as the study of preventive medicine is to physical health. The fact that preventive medicine is written about and discussed more than preventive law does not mean that the law is less important. Nor does it help, in the day of trouble, to explain that the theatre manager or owner did not understand that there was a legal problem which could have been understood earlier by getting competent legal advice. Such ignorance may be an explanation, but in the eyes of the law it will not pass for an excuse. Many of us get the habit of thinking that if we tend to our own business, we won't get into trouble. If this idea was ever true, it is now false and out of date. Today one does not have to be doing something to get into legal trouble; he may get into it just as quickly and just as seriously by doing nothing, by waiting, or by postponing.

It is true in theatre activities as in personal experiences that we cannot foresee certain embarrassing problems and we refer to these as "tough breaks." However, most of our problems do not suddenly appear, full-grown. Usually they have small beginnings and their incipient growth should be a cue for preventive action.

It is not possible in a short or a long chapter to review all the laws governing theatres. Legal aspects of the field are far too extensive and conditions too varied and changing to be covered. The entrance of radio and television into the field of entertainment has had far-reaching effects. Every state has its own code, which differs from that of the other forty nine. Cities within a state may also have different regulations. For example, in New York City, where theatre problems are extremely complicated, the laws would be different from those of Albany or Buffalo. If each manager would familiarize himself with the laws of his own state and city, he would be doing well.

Some theatres have on their board of directors a lawyer who keeps an eye on all legal aspects. This is a simple and timely expedient for having legal counsel constantly on tap. Other theatres have a lawyer on a retaining fee.

Authority to Regulate

It may be helpful to consider a few general statements as recorded in *American Jurisprudence* (1944), Volume 58:

In general, the power and authority to regulate theatres and places of amusement, includes the power to control and supervise them in all matters which are essential to the public peace, morals, safety, health and sanitation and convenience, subject to the qualifications that the city has no power, under the guise of fixing permissible locations, entirely to exclude from the city limits a particular kind of amusement.

The rule that an owner or occupant of land or building who invites or induces others to go thereon or therein, owes to those who do so a duty to have and keep his premises in reasonably safe condition applies to theatres and public amusements.

Duties and Liability of Owners and Proprietors

The division of law regarding the manager's or owner's responsibility for the safety and well-being of the customers is discussed at greater length and detail than any other phase of theatre law and operation. The discussion and cases on safety are given much greater attention than the entertainment to be presented. There is frequent repetition of such comments as this, "Theatre patrons are entitled to full protection at the hands of managers of the theatre in the enjoyment of the privilege for which they have paid money." Considerable emphasis is placed on the fact that a manager has made an effort to bring people to his theatre. For instance, "One who purchases a ticket and attends a theatre is an invitee, within the full legal meaning of the term, as distinguished from a licensee. Where there is some benefit to the invitor, his duty to exercise care and to have his premises safe is increased" (*American Jurisprudence*).

It is doubtful that many managers would realize or believe that they have a responsibility for the protection of the patrons with regard to each other. For instance, the owner or proprietor of a theatre of public amusement is liable for assault or abuse of a patron, as well as for injuries suffered by the patron as the result of acts or conduct of other patrons. So the proprietor may find himself in the role of a peacemaker if he wants to get along well in his business. "Blessed are the peacemakers for they shall be called the children of God."

Overcrowding the theatre. Many theatre managers would like to be troubled with problems of overcrowding; crowds are usually too small. The problems of overcrowding, however, can be something to worry about. It is interesting to note that there is no edict against overcrowding itself, but failure to take care of the crowds may create a liability. There definitely is a duty to avoid dangers which may arise in the entrances and the exits. If there is negligence on the part of the manager with regard to crowd control, he is culpable; but the presence of a very large crowd is unobjectionable.

It is important that hallways and aisles be kept free from obstructions. A portable chair placed in the aisle is generally forbidden by law. Even if it were not forbidden, the management should recognize that such an obstruction could be dangerous unless it were most cautiously taken care of. The practice of putting in a whole row of movable chairs is highly questionable.

Contributory negligence. It sometimes happens that patrons of the theatre themselves get into difficulties because they do not exercise reasonable care. This lack of care is referred to as contributory negligence, and if such is proved the manager of the theatre cannot be held responsible. To illustrate this point, the following two cases are cited: A theatre owner was not responsible to a patron who fell down a flight of stairs in the balcony when the patron was merely informed by an usher that there were "better seats in the balcony," and, according to testimony of the patron, there was sufficient light to enable her to see the steps and that the latter were alternately narrow and wide. The court distinguished this situation from one arising in a case where the patron was told by the usher to "go to the balcony," which was dimly lighted. There the court held the patron was free from contributory negligence. The line between the two is rather clear-cut, in that the patron in the first case was partially at fault or negligent.

Insufficient illumination. Because proper stage effects depend on stage lighting, it is necessary to work with reduced light in the theatre proper or auditorium. But if the light is too dim at the top of a stairway for people to see a four-inch depression on the floor (a step), it may be validly contended that there was negligence. The theatre manager or owner is duty bound to light the aisles and stairways sufficiently. A dispute as to whether or not a section of the theatre wherein a plaintiff was injured was sufficiently lighted is an issue for the jury.

Minor Problems of Safety for the Patrons. Loose boards, worn and torn rugs, broken steps, trap doors, doors locked that should be open, doors open that should be locked, broken seats, and slick floors are a constant worry of the theatre manager. If the owner or manager does not know about a problem because it has developed so recently that he has not had time to know of it, he may not be guilty of negligence, but if he has had sufficient time to know of it and has not taken steps to correct it, he is guilty of negligence. As a matter of safety routine, the theatre should be examined daily and all necessary repairs and corrections taken care of immediately.

Theatre tickets—What are they? There are different versions as to just what a ticket represents. In some places it is regarded as a mere license, revocable at the will of the proprietor or the theatre. In other places it is an irrevocable license, provided that the ticket holder does not create a disturbance or engage in some other illegal activity. It is regarded as a kind of contract for a theatre seat, in a certain place in the theatre during the performance named on the ticket and at the hour, day and place designated on said ticket. If the manager of the theatre changes any item listed on the ticket which the purchaser does not wish to accept he may request a refund. For instance, if the play was changed from *Our Town* to *Street Scene,* and the patron did not wish to accept the substitution, he could legally request a refund. If the ticket which he bought gave no name but merely listed the note, "to be selected," and *Street Scene* was later chosen, he could not legally request a refund. Of course, the manager may make a refund in order to keep the customer's

good will or for some other reason, but he would have no legal obligation to do so.

Although the protection of a ticket holder is thoroughgoing, he cannot
be allowed to annoy or disturb others. The management has the right to
ask anyone who is disturbing others to desist or leave, providing this is
done without causing unnecessary humiliation. Care should be taken to
make sure that the particular person addressed is really guilty of improper conduct; and if it becomes necessary to evict anyone from the
place, care should be taken not to use more force than is reasonably necessary. The superintendent of the theatre owes a duty to the patrons to
maintain order and quiet during a performance.

Operation of the coat or checkroom. It is common practice for theatres
to operate a checkroom in or adjacent to the lobby. For such a service
there is usually a few cents charge on each article such as hat, cloak,
coat, or umbrella. Sometimes, however, the service is free, which actually
means that it is included in the price of the show ticket. A claim check
with identical numbers on each end is used for identification. One half
is attached to the article and the other half given to the patron as a
reclaim check.

In some smaller theatres, a room or hallway is provided where people
may hang up or deposit their own wraps as they enter and pick them
up as they leave. There is usually no charge for this service and no special
attendant is present. It is surprising to learn that users of this service
report very little trouble with it. The Lion House in Salt Lake City, Utah,
boasts that it handles thousands of items each week by this system, and
has never known of a lost item.

Perhaps everyone has stood before a check stand while questions such
as these went through his mind: "I wonder how reliable this place is?
How safe will my property be if I leave it here? Will someone go through
all the pockets? Will the wraps be all wrinkled and messed up as if they
had been jammed in a small box? What would happen if they could not
find my property when I called for it?"

Let us first answer the questions in a general way and then discuss
some of the legal explanations.

(1) If the check stand is operated as a business venture for financial
benefit of the operator, the patron has greater assurance that his property
will be protected, because the operator has greater liability. If he decided

to put up a sign. "Not responsible for loss by fire or theft," the sign would not clear him of responsibility for safe return of the property.

(2) If the service is operated for mutual benefit of the patron as well as the operator, so that one makes a little money and the other enjoys the convenience to the extent that it is a kind of fifty-fifty arrangement, then the liability is not so emphatic and the property would be somewhat less secure.

(3) If the checking service existed entirely for the benefit of the patron and represented little or no value to the operator, the liability would be proportionately less and the service might be slight.

The degree of care and thoroughness shown in being responsible for the items assigned to the check stand is the all-important consideration.

A little understanding of the legal interpretations of such services may add some light; however, the problems are seldom clean cut, nor are terms clearly defined. Often the terms are so vague and loose as to have little meaning. The operation of a theatre check stand comes under the division of law known as *bailment* as it concerns personal property.

Under this classification, bailments are divided into three classes: (1) those which benefit the bailee, the person who takes care of the check stand, or his employer; (2) those bailments wherein the benefit of the transaction is reciprocal or to mutual advantage; (3) bailment for the benefit of the bailor, who is the owner of the property or bailment. In this, the bailee performs a gratuitous service for the bailor.

In each case some degree of care is expected, and it is this degree which is the real test. Gross negligence is the failure to use slight care; slight negligence is the failure to use great care; and ordinary negligence is, of course, the failure to use ordinary care. When one attempts to amplify these terms, he is likely to pick up another list of words equally ambiguous and vague. "Gross negligence" would of course be greater in magnitude than "negligence," but it might be less than "willful, wanton, and intentional negligence."

One closing thought: the bailee is not an insurer of the goods and cannot be held liable for their damage or destruction unless guilty of some fault of omission or commission.

Does the following story have any point of value? A large department store once extended the unusual service of tending babies while their mothers shopped. As the babies were checked in, each mother was given a claim check which she most positively would have to present to reclaim her baby. One day a lady lost her claim check. She pleaded with the attendant to let her have her baby, but it was to no avail—she must produce the claim check. If she could not do that, she would have to wait until all other babies had been reclaimed and then take the one which was left. This she did because it was the only thing she could do. When the mother appeared at closing time to get the last infant, the attendant brought her a little colored child—which provided a happy ending, for the mother herself was colored.

Proper incorporation for nonprofit theatres. Experienced legal advisers have called attention to certain protective measures which theatre boards in all states should understand clearly.

The members of an unincorporated theatre are personally liable for neglect or intentional wrong to a customer by one of the officers of the association. Therefore, it is recommended that the theatre should incorporate under the nonprofit corporation law of the state in which it is operated. This would free all members from personal liability except the member or officer who was personally negligent or a willful wrong-doer as an agent of the corporation.

However, if the theatre is a division of the state university or college, which share immunity from tort liability because it is a division of the state, it is neither necessary nor appropriate to incorporate such theatre organization.

On the other hand, a municipality is responsible for torts committed by its agents in the course of their employment. These would include theatres organized and operating as a division of a city high school existing as a division of an incorporated school district or in a similar position legally as a high school municipality. In other words, they do not share immunity from tort liability as do colleges and universities which are legal persons partaking of the sovereignty of the state itself.

The importance of proper insurance. Under present conditions no theatre should attempt operation without adequate insurance. The cost of a single accident could bankrupt a theatre. Moreover, the laws in most states are such that it would be impossible to operate without insurance. It is strongly recommended that careful study be made of basic insurances.

A service of great value in this regard is presented in a pamphlet circulated by American National Theatre and Academy (ANTA), 1545 Broadway, New York. It was prepared by Harry M. Simon and F. J. Turner, theatre insurance specialists, and is called a "Summary of Basic Insurances to Cover Production Operation by a Resident Theatre." Following are some of the important items of that study. Space does not permit the complete reproduction, but it can be obtained from ANTA.

Public liability. This coverage should be on the Comprehensive General Liability form which will protect the producer-owner's legal liability for bodily injury or death caused to the public and damage to property of the public. The limits should be $200,000 for one person injured or killed in an accident with a minimum secondary limit of $500,000 for more than one person injured or killed in the same accident; secondary limits of $1 million per accident may be advisable because of catastrophe resulting from fire or other causes, particularly if exits are not plentiful and properly noted. The coverage should provide protection against an "occurrence" instead of "accident," as "occurrence" gives the broadest possible concept for claim coverage, whereas the word "accident" limits to an accident, a fortuitous event.

The premium rate is based upon the number of admissions, paid or otherwise. Minimum limits for property damage of $5,000 per accident with aggregate coverage of $25,000 for all claims are recommended.

(a) *Backstage Parties.* We caution against holding parties back stage in celebration of the run of a play or in testimony to a star. Frequently, especially if liquor is served, an occurrence may develop for which you could be liable.

(b) *Coat Room Legal Liability.* If coats and other property are checked, the producer may be held responsible under the law of the particular state in which the theatre is located. If so, insurance covering checkroom legal liability is recommended.

(c) *Products Liability.* This form is needed if candy, drinks, sandwiches, and other food are sold.

Compensation Insurance. This is mandatory in most states, but it is questionable whether nonprofit organizations must carry insurance.

Theatrical Floater. The physical production, consisting of scenery, costumes, sets, and other theatrical properties, should be insured under a theatrical floater form.

Burglary and Holdup Insurance. Insurance should be carried to cover all money in the box office, also while kept overnight in the safe and while being taken to and from the bank, also including employees' payrolls.

Libel Insurance. The question of libel insurance, including invasion of sanctity, has become increasingly pressing, with suits being brought against playwrights, producers, and theatre owners.

XIV

HELPFUL BOOKS AND PERIODICALS

There are a few books and periodicals which are extremely helpful in providing authentic answers to theatre problems. The question and answer treatment is aimed to provide cues and leads as to where one may find the answers.

Books

Best Plays of 1960–1961, The
  (or any year since 1899)
Dodd Mead and Company
New York, New York

. . . answers these and other important questions:
1. Where can I find a condensation of the actual dialogue from the best plays of a given year? (This source gives an abridgment.)
2. Where can I find a roundup of what happened in the theatre in London, Chicago, Paris, and New York last year? (This source gives a complete report.)
3. Is there a list of the most famous long-run plays produced on Broadway with the length of time for each run? (Yes, it is a feature of the last part of the book.)
4. Are not the Pulitzer Prize Plays and the New York Critics' Circle awards almost identical? (No, they are widely different. Both lists are given in the last part of this source.)
5. Can I find a list of all the Broadway plays and musicals with the casts and other information? (Yes, this reference has all that and it also

gives the number of performances that were given to each production.)

> Note: This collection of plays is commonly referred to as *Burns Mantle Plays* because Mr. Mantle was its famous editor and critic from 1919 until his death in 1949.

Community Theatre and How It Works, The
John Wray Young
Harper & Brothers, Publishers
New York, New York

. . . . answers these and other important questions
1. How have successful community theatres been organized? (Chapter Two.)
2. By what means have community theatres come to own their own theatres? (Chapter Seven.)
3. Why do community theatres fail? (Chapter Five.)
4. Is there danger of shocking the audience right out of the auditorium? (Real danger, Chapter Nine.)
5. What community groups should a theatre represent? (Chapter Seven.)
6. What has experience taught us about seating arrangement in the theatre? (Chapter Seven.)

Curtains Going Up
Albert McCleery and Carl Glick
Pitman Publishing Corporation
New York, New York

. . . answers these and other important questions:
1. What is a community theatre and what is the need for one when there is so much professional theatre? (Foreword.)
2. Is there a brief, concise history of community theatres in America? (Yes, page 325.)
3. What procedures have been followed in organizing community theatres, and where can I get information on organizing one in my area? (Descriptive reports on all areas are recorded throughout the book.)
4. Are "little theatres" organized on a national basis? (Page 351.)

5. What details should be included in a constitution and by-laws for a "little theatre" organization? (Page 372.)
6. Can I find a breakdown of receipts and disbursements for the operation of an average community theatre? (Yes, page 386.)
7. In what ways are community theatres financed? (See reports from various areas.)
8. Is there a list of rules available for judging a play tournament? (Yes, pages 381–384.)
9. Who are some of the leaders, organizers, and directors of community theatres? (See reports from various areas.)
10. Can I find a list of community theatres arranged by states? (Yes, page 367.)

Directory of Newspapers and
Periodicals
Published annually by N. W. Ayer & Son, Inc.
Philadelphia 6, Pennsylvania
(This book has special value for traveling shows).

. . . answers these and other important questions:
1. Is there a detailed, scaled map available of individual states and Canadian provinces? (Throughout Ayer's Directory there are detailed maps of the United States and Canadian provinces.)
2. Where can one find information as to the estimated population, and increases and decreases of population of states and provinces in the United States and Canada? (Look under the specific name of state or province.)
3. What authentic, condensed information is available about cities and towns of the United States and Canada as to population, manufacturing, and industries? (Complete information on each city is listed.)
4. In preparing theatre publicity, where can I find out how many newspapers are in my area, and what it costs to advertise in them? (Cities of the area in which you are interested carry full details.)
5. Are there any newspapers or periodicals that will not accept advertising? (Yes, a few. Description of each paper gives this information.)
6. How could I determine the earnings per capita in my state? (Earnings per capita are listed for each state.)

7. Is there a complete compilation of every kind of publication, grouped according to classification, such as dailies, college, religious, and weeklies, that are printed in the United States and Canada? (Last page of book.)
8. In mapping out a selling campaign, how could I find out what transportation facilities serve a certain city and surrounding area? (Public transportation is listed for every city.)

Encyclopedia of Exploitation, The
Bill Hendricks and Howard Waugh
Showmen's Trade Review
New York, New York

. . . answers these and other important questions:
1. Is there an over-all list of tricks and "gimmicks" for show selling? (Yes, this book gives over 1,000.)
2. How can a display of false teeth be used to promote a comedy? (Page 193.)
3. Bookmarks and blotters are inexpensive, but how valuable and effective are they in theatre advertising? (Page 126.)
4. Is an animated sign worth the extra price? (Yes, page 429.)
5. To increase ticket sales, would a "gimmick" such as a beauty contest ever be justified? (See page 41.)

An Introduction To The Theatre
Frank M. Whiting
Harper & Brothers, Publishers
New York, New York

. . . . answers these and other questions:
1. Is financial success closely related to scenic design? (Chapter 10.)
2. Are there many good plays with limited scenery? (Yes, some, but see Chapter 10.)
3. Why are there more successful symphony orchestras in our country than successful theatres? (Read "Theatre as a Profession.")
4. Are professional actors financially secure? (ibid.)
5. What is the status of the much discussed move to decentralize the theatre? (ibid.)

Film Daily Year Book, The
Published annually by the Film Daily
New York, New York

. . . answers these and other important questions:

1. What were the ten best plays of the year according to box office standards? (First pages.)
2. Where can I find a list of the theatres in my area, along with the number of people they seat? (Capacities of movie theatres are listed by states.)
3. Who are some of the acting stars of the year, and some featured performers? (Found in Academy Awards' section.)
4. Is there a list of motion pictures produced over a period of years? (Yes, over 25,000 titles of movies since 1915.)

Guide to Great Plays, A
Joseph T. Shipley
Public Affairs Press (1956)
Washington, D.C.

. . . answers these and other important questions:

1. Where can I find a comprehensive, up-to-date list of the great plays of all time from all countries? (This book records nearly a thousand such plays.)
2. Is there a reference book that gives a synopsis of each of the great plays? (Yes, this book gives some high points.)
3. Is it possible to find important aspects of a play's history? (Yes. This book gives data on first performances and public interest.)

Masterplots
Frank Magill
Salem Press, Inc.
New York 17, New York

. . . answers these and other important questions:

1. For publicity use I want the condensed story of a great play, e.g., *Ghosts,* along with information on author and principal characters. (It is alphabetically listed by title.)

2. Where can I find a reliable critique of a great play? (Each play has a good critique.)
3. Is there a complete commentary on classical and well known modern plays? (No, but this source covers a great many and covers them well.)

New York Theatre Critics' Reviews
Critics' Theatre Reviews
New York 10, New York

. . . answers these and other important questions:
1. I want to get the original reviews of a Broadway musical, i.e., *My Fair Lady*. Will I have to go to the originals to get them? (No, Critics Reviews has compiled major New York newspaper reviews in one group.)
2. Is there an up-to-date listing of the Broadway producers, scenic designers, stage directors, costumers, authors, composers, and actors? (Yes, it is compiled annually in Critics' Reviews.)
3. Do the critics usually tell the plot of a play in their review of it? (They often do, but the synopsis is very brief.)
4. Are long-run plays often given more than one review? (Yes, especially if there are changes in cast or other important changes.)

Showmanship in Advertising
Bill Hendricks and Montgomery Orr
Showmen's Trade Review
New York 18, New York

. . . answers these and other important questions:
1. What items of information must be included in a theatre newspaper advertisement? (Page 5.)
2. I want to use color for emphasis, but how will I know what to use and when? (Page 55.)
3. Do different styles and sizes of type tell the story more effectively? (Yes, page 77.)
4. Is there a chart showing the meaning of proofreader's marks? (Yes, page 88.)
5. Where can I find out about the various printing processes, such as offset, letterpress, and lithography? (Page 93.)

6. What are some of the important basic rules for constructing and "laying out" newspaper ads? (Pages 10 and 149.)
7. In making budget allotments for advertising, what items should be covered? (Page 183.)
8. Would holidays and seasonal occasions suggest special copy for my theatre advertising layouts? (Yes, page 210.)
9. Are there idea suggestions for ads? If so, how can I gather and utilize such reference material? (Page 210.)
10. How can I determine the best sales slant to get the maximum out of my advertising dollar? (Page 101.)

Simon's Directory of Theatrical Materials,
Services & Information
Bernard Simon
New York 19, New York

. . . answers these and other important questions:
1. Where can I find a list of costume houses in various parts of the country?
2. Is there an agency which prepares "package" publicity for current popular plays?
3. Can I find a list of the various play writing competitions, with information about the contest? Can I find the name and address of the person in charge?
4. Are there several different companies that handle a complete line of stage equipment, such as draperies, dimmers, and lights?
5. Where can I find distributors of records for various types of sound effects, such as thunder, howling dogs, and sounds of wild beasts?

Note: All information is alphabetically listed by subject.

Tested Sentences That Sell
Elmer Wheeler
Prentice - Hall, Inc.
New York, New York
. . . answers these and other important questions:
1. Is there a tested sentence structure that makes a prospective buyer say "yes"? (Page 25 and 77.)

2. Can I find examples of right and wrong approaches to improve my selling technique? (Yes, page 110.)
3. What type of appeal would put my customer at ease when I deliver my sales pitch? (Page 87.)
4. Are "oddities" effective in a selling approach? (Yes, page 174.)
5. Where can I find an idea on word combination that would be helpful at the ticket office? (Page 31.)
6. What helps in word phrasing can I find to make my advertising "catchy"? (Page 28.)
7. Are there suggestions for helping the patron make decisions as to the price of tickets and even the choice of performance? (Yes, page 75.)
8. Why is it better to give the patron a choice between something and something instead of a choice between something and nothing? (Page 15.)

Theatre Handbook (1950 Edition)
Bernard Sobel
Crown Publishers
New York, New York

. . . answers these and other important questions:
1. Where can I find an article on theatre critics and criticisms? (Page 193.)
2. Where can I find practical suggestions for press agents? (Page 632.)
3. Is there a list of the best known community theatres? (Yes, page 492.)
4. I need a brief biography of a famous actor or playwright, e.g., George Bernard Shaw. (Page 703.)
5. If a play is copyrighted in the United States for twenty-eight years plus one renewal, does it then become public property free for all use? (Yes, page 179.)
6. Are some of Shaw's plays out of copyright in the United States? (Yes, all of his plays which were written before 1904 are free. Page 703.)
7. Where can I find a condensed story of any great play, e.g., *The Rivals*, by Sheridan? (Page 667.)
8. Is there a list of Pulitzer Prize plays? (Yes, page 645.)
9. Where can I find an excellent bibliography on the theatre, such as

acting, staging, anthologies of plays, biography, dramatic technique, lighting, make-up, costuming, and scenery? (Page 867.)

10. Is there a list of plays arranged by subjects, for instance, plays about adultery or adolescence? (Yes, Pages 277–295.)

Theatres and Auditoriums
Harold Burris-Meyer and Edward C. Cole
Reinhold
New York, New York

. . . answers these and other important questions:

1. Approaching the problem of audience accommodation, where can I find practical, tested information on planning a theatre auditorium? (Pages 31–73.)
2. In planning control of audience traffic, what specific items such as parking facilities should be considered? (Page 16.)
3. Basically, what constitutes the various types of stage structures and scenery? (Page 74–109.)
4. What is the interrelationship of the various theatrical functions such as script preparation, rehearsals, and production? (Page 203.)
5. Where can I obtain practical instruction about the mechanics of light and sound for background and settings? (Pages 155–184.)

Periodicals

Dramatics
Published monthly during school by
The National Thespian Society
College Hill Station
Cincinnati 24, Ohio

. . . answers these and other important questions:

1. Can I find out what plays are being produced most often this season in the high schools? (Yes, it keeps you up to date.)
2. Is there information available about current children's theatre pro-productions? (Each issue has a "Theatre for Children.")
3. Can I find practical helps in production problems about furniture and hand props, costuming, and set designing? (A series of helpful articles on these topics is included in the magazine.)

4. What plays are currently being presented at the different Broadway theatres? (Each issue carries a complete list.)

5. Is there a list of scheduled theatre conferences in different parts of the country? (Yes, information is given on conferences.)

Educational Theatre Journal
Published quarterly for the
American Educational Theatre Association
University of Minnesota, Minneapolis 14

. . . answers these and other important questions:

1. Where can I find a current list of the officers of the AETA? (Yes, *ETJ* has it.)

2. How many American universities give doctor's degrees in theatre? (More than twenty. See graduate theses.)

3. Are allied arts of the theatre given study by national leaders of educational theatre? (Yes, reports are published in *ETJ*.)

New Yorker, The
Published weekly by
The New Yorker Magazine, Inc.
25 W. 43rd St.
New York 36, New York

. . . answers these and other important questions:

1. Does *The New Yorker* give a list of current stage shows on Broadway? (Yes, just inside the front cover.)

2. Can you get an idea of what the plays are about? (Yes, the idea of each one is concisely stated.)

3. Is there a critique of the plays listed? (Yes, brief but good.)

4. Are starting time and days of performances given? (Yes, also location and telephone number of theatre.)

5. Does the periodical carry a discussion of allied arts? (It has information on movies, music, and books.)

Players Magazine
Published monthly, October through May, by
National Collegiate Players
Box 339
Gainesville, Florida

. . . answers these and other important questions:
1. Where can I find information on activities of college theatres? (Excellent articles are presented here.)
2. Is there a list of plays currently being produced by colleges, high schools, and communities? (Yes, hundreds are so listed.)
3. I need to find names of firms who specialize in lighting equipment, costumes, and theatre needs. (All such firms advertise here.)

Quarterly Journal of Speech
Published by
Speech Association of America
Bloomington, Indiana

. . . answers these and other important questions:
1. To what extent does the National Speech Association recognize drama and theatre in its official journal? (Extensively—several articles in each issue.)
2. What is the working relationship of speech and theatre among leading universities? (Some are independent, and some are in speech departments.)
3. Where are new theatre books listed and completely reviewed? (New books in review are in *QJ*.)
4. In the field of educational theatre, where does one find thorough and scholarly essays? (*QJ* has held for scholarly standards all the way.)

Theatre Arts
Published monthly
1545 Broadway
New York, New York

. . . answers these and other important questions:
1. What are the current plays on Broadway, their casts, directors, and plot summaries? (See the current issue of *TA*.)

2. Where can I find a complete calendar of theatre productions on Broadway, off Broadway, and in all the states? (*TA* calendar.)
3. What operas are playing where today? (See "Opera House" section.)
4. Where can I buy theatre equipment? (See any *TA* issue.)
5. What are the names of some good drama schools? (See advertisements.)
6. What are theatres in the United States doing in the way of new ventures, new plays, and touring abroad? (See "Theatre USA" section.)

Variety
Published weekly by
Variety, Inc.
154 West 46th Street
New York, New York

. . . answers these and other important questions:
1. Where can I find business news on current theatre, movies, radio, TV, legitimate stage, vaudeville, and music? (*Variety* gives it all.)
2. Can I find out how long a Broadway show has been playing, and how much money the box office took in last week? (See "Legitimate" section.)
3. What are the seating capacities of the Broadway theatres? (See "Legitimate" section on Broadway reports.)
4. What shows are playing on the London stage, and how are they faring? (Well reported in *Variety*.)
5. What is now happening to the movie business in various parts of the country? ("Pictures" has a big section.)
6. What is the trend in radio listening today? (See "Radio-Television" section.)
7. What are the top song hits of the week? (Top records, sheet music, and coin machines reported in the "Music" section.)

XV

MONEY-SAVING DEVICES

The old proverb, "A penny saved is a penny earned" makes no exception of the theatre. The ability to save a little on a number of things may make the difference as to whether a theatre stays in business or closes its doors. Some of the most original, imaginative, and interesting people are in the theatre. Audiences literally gasp at the scenic effects they create. Most theatre people have learned the need of economy; that is, most of them who are still in business. They know that to keep the theatre going they have to train free help, make things over, wear things out, rebuild, and improvise. They have fun doing it, for this is their art, their relaxation, and amusement. It would be impossible to even list the many little ways that theatres devise to save money, but two major ones which are not so well known are presented on the following pages.

Dr. Ralph Margetts, of the University of Utah, comes from a distinguished theatre family. His versatility and training have made him fully aware of theatre problems, especially technical problems. Over the years he has made a hobby of creating stage properties and accessories at an absolute minimum cost. Through his imagination and his ability to make the complex seem simple, he has been able to save the theatre thousands of dollars and give it an amazing richness and authority. The author persuaded Dr. Margetts to write up some of his most effective money-saving ideas especially for this publication.

A "Prop" for the Fainting Budget

The art of dollar-stretching can be practiced best in theatres where there is cooperation between the business manager and the various divisions of production. An alert manager plugs many financial leaks of which his associates, absorbed in their own affairs, are completely oblivious. But even the most astute manager cannot control the operations of the property department. Stage properties will be costly or inexpensive depending upon the character of the property manager.

Wanted—a wizard. Every amateur theatre should seek out a man for this job who has the ingenuity of Thomas A. Edison and the soul of a miser. It has become axiomatic in the nonprofessional theatre for the property department to refrain from spending money on anything which could be begged, borrowed, or stolen. Since the eighth commandment of the Decalogue specifically forbids stealing, and borrowing "dulls the edge of husbandry," and, since the proverb, "The Lord helps those who help themselves," has never been really understood, a more ethical method of procurement must be devised. In college theatres all over the country there are gifted artisans who have developed inexpensive ways of providing stage properties. While there are individual differences in method, they all amount to what I shall call the *make-and-fake theory of stage properties.*

The devaluated dollar may be made of silver, but it might as well be quicksilver the way it slips through the fingers. The make-and-fake method offers a way to stabilize this illusive element by making it amalgamate with the gold of ingenuity.

Genuine fakes. Most directors suffer from the mistaken belief that the exact article called for by the script is best for the show. It is true that properties should fit and not obtrude upon the scene, but it is also true that there is a certain magnification, especially upon very large stages, which demands judicious exaggeration. Frequently a manufactured property is more effective than the real thing. For example, a beautiful antique dagger was needed for an outdoor production of *Samson and Delilah.* Clara Mae Turner, singing the role of the biblical temptress, was horrified at the crudity of an enormous wooden dagger presented her by the prop man. From the distant audience, however, that painted wooden atrocity was perfect.

There is a distinct relationship between genuine furniture and painted scenery. The inadequacies of the latter are accentuated by the proximity of the former: a beautifully finished piece of furniture on the stage tends to emphasize by its excellence the imperfections of the scenery behind it. While an audience may be willing to "suspend disbelief," it cannot disconnect subconscious comparison. Therefore, a hand-rubbed mahogany wall bracket attached to a simulated mahogany panel will shriek, "one of us is a fake." Conversely, a shelf made of even scrap lumber found in the scene shop and painted with the same paint as the scenery will retire into the background and assume its proper function as a part of the decor of the set.

Borrowing and sorrowing. The time-honored custom of borrowing furniture for stage productions is fraught with hazards to both "him that gives and him that takes." Good property men, of course, always return borrowed furniture, but there are times when they hesitate to face the owners. Explaining how an irreplaceable antique has been burned by a carelessly placed cigarette or damaged by an inept handler is an unpleasant task. Business managers have watched their meagre profits dwindle and disappear in reimbursement checks to aggrieved lenders. Worst of all, damaging of borrowed articles results in bad public relations. It is especially unfortunate because much of the budget drain occasioned by lost or broken props can be avoided.

The nerve strain attendant upon the production of any play is sufficient in itself without the added worry of caring for borrowed furniture. It is always desirable, if not always possible, to own the furniture used on the stage. But just how is this done? There are at least two methods of building up the furniture section of any property department which do not involve serious expenditures from the budget: furniture may be acquired outright by the theatre, or by the make-and-fake method.

The art of acquisition. The method of outright acquisition is the first suggestion. Because of various unpredictable factors, settings are rarely dressed until the last possible moment, and the provident property master, realizing the possibility of last-minute demands, must be prepared for them. If he is wise, he will stockpile old furniture in the nooks and crannies of the theatre as a reserve against such contingencies.

"Oh! yeah!" comes the inevitable question, "and just where does all this furniture come from?"

Well, hidden away in many attics and basements are countless specimens of old furniture. Secretly, most of the owners would be happy to get rid of these white elephants, especially if they believed that they might serve a worthy cause and if someone would haul them away. Try putting an advertisement in the newspaper, and bill your request for contributions of old furniture as a worthy cause, which it is, and see how many contributors you will find. It is then a simple matter to hire a truck and pick up the loot. Furniture thus acquired can be rebuilt, repainted, or reupholstered to suit the theatre's need. You get what many believe would be impossible to find simply because you ask for it.

Build it yourself. Period furniture is more difficult to obtain, so use the make-and-fake method. The standard furnishings of an Elizabethan drama, for example, such as stools, benches, chairs, tables, and thrones can be made both cheaply and quickly in any well-appointed scene shop. With just a few power tools, a band saw, a table saw, and a drill press, almost any piece of furniture can be made or faked. If there is a set of dado heads for the table saw, a wonderful assortment of fancy trims is possible. Massive tables like the one used for the feast in *Macbeth* are found only in conference rooms, and are rarely loaned. Even if such a loan could be negotiated, the cost of transportation and handling, not to mention the risk of damage, would be more than the cost of materials with which to build a replica. Heavy legs or end supports can be hollow. Carvings can be plywood cut out and glued to the surface, and the heavy slab top may be faked by a plain or shaped edging of wood. If you can find a plain door, you have a ready-made table top. A highly polished finish can be quickly had by applying two coats of quick-drying shellac. The first coat should be thoroughly dry before the second is applied; otherwise the surface will always be faintly sticky.

Probably the most useful piece of stage furniture is the bench-stool. A usable design can be found in any good text on the history of furniture and the stool can be reproduced in quantity. One of the advantages of this type of furniture is that it may be tossed about. If it gets broken, make another. Artistic expression is thus liberated. Should the director feel that a scene would be more effective if one actor chucked a stool at another actor's head, he can dismiss all consideration for the stool and worry about his actor's skull.

Useful chairs. The common straight chair is one need of the theatre not readily supplied by either of the methods previously mentioned. If any single chair could be recommended as being most suited to the stage, it could only be the ubiquitous bentwood. Ruggedly built, it withstands rough usage without distress and is efficient, light, and unobtrusive. Gilded, the bentwood presents a reasonable facsimile of a gold chair. Since its use is so widespread, it may not be difficult for most theatres to borrow. If not, it can be rented, but remember that a couple of rentals will equal the purchase price.

Drapes and curtains. Most interior settings are incomplete without drapes and curtains. Draperies, their acquisition or fabrication, must be made to fit into our formula somewhere, but as every woman knows who has decorated her own home, curtains and drapes are costly items. Furthermore, quite apart from their cost, they must be carefully selected to harmonize with the furnishings of the room represented.

How can a theatre provide enough variety of acceptable drapes for a season of plays without repeating the hangings until the audience is overfamiliar with each fabric and design? Perhaps the lend-lease technique might be employed to augment the supply—lend-lease, in this case, being the well-established custom of pillaging the homes of all members of the property crew. Beware of this, however, for even the most indulgent parents may eventually object to living in curtainless rooms while their drapes are being ogled by audiences of the local little theatre group.

What is the answer to this problem? Muslin, the universal cloth of the stage, can be persuaded to masquerade as brocade, velour, drapery material, in fact almost anything desired. For instance, suppose that in a modernistic setting a subtle candy stripe drape would fit the room. Don't rush out and buy a maroon and cream silk at nine dollars a yard. Just staple a couple of yards of muslin on a work bench and paint stripes on it with a rubber base paint. When they are hung on the set under lights, they will pass for silk very nicely. Should a design of some sort be needed the silk screen method can be used to apply it. An attractive set of draw curtains was made for the setting of *Affairs of State* in this way. Unbleached muslin was first spattered with yellow; then a composite design of the three most prominent architectural features of Washington D. C.—the White House, the Lincoln Memorial, and the Washington Monument—were stenciled on in pale green using the silk-screen method. The total cost, including the material was less than five dollars. Probably the greatest advantage, aside from the low cost, is the infinite variety of drapes made possible by this method. Even when the play closes its run, the curtains are not a loss, for the muslin can then be used to cover flats or pad platforms.

Small props and hand props. The scope of responsibility assigned to the property department is disconcertingly broad. When the set has been dressed to the satisfaction of director and producer, the prop crew must turn its attention to the myriad hand props which playwrights toss nonchalantly into their scripts. Why shouldn't they? They do not have to find them. If by some miracle the author has practiced restraint in this regard, the director may be moved to add some of his own devising to enliven the scene. It is an old theatrical trick to rescue tedious passages with parades, using banners, organ-grinders, or pushcart hawkers.

The catalogue of hand properties which could be required in the theatre staggers the imagination. To discuss them all would be useless. But, the more commonly-used props should be considered, for they can be made inexpensively if inventiveness, imagination, and persistence characterize those charged with the responsibility of propping the show. Any of the following props, for instance, can be manufactured in the scene shop: spears, daggers, swords, lanterns, banners, rifles, pistols, garlands, flowers, goblets, and a host of others.

Safety first. As specific examples, let's consider spears, goblets, daggers and guns. These are undoubtedly needed as often as any hand props.

Every aspiring actor has carried spears at some time in his career. Rented from a costumer, spears for one Shakespeare play will gash any budget. But why rent when the materials to make them can be bought for the same price or less? Every lumber yard in America carries a supply of 1⅜" full round in 16' lengths. Here are inexpensive hafts for spears. Spearheads of any design, no matter how intricate, can be cut from ¼" plywood and fitted to the haft. From the simple Roman javelin to fancy English and French halberds, a wide variety of designs can be found under "weapons" in a good encyclopedia. Head and haft fastened together with small nails or glue, painting the head with aluminum paint is a matter of a few moments' work. For the haft use burnt sienna water paint rather than black, which has a tendency to smear. The result is a very creditable stage spear. For those who crave realism sheet aluminum is available for the spearheads; it can be sawed like wood on a band saw with a skip-tooth blade. If aluminum is used, however, the cost of the spears will be considerably greater.

Is this a dagger?—Heaven forbid! Daggers may be made in much the same way as spears. If you are lucky enough to find either an old chair with intricately turned legs and rungs or some old balusters which are sufficiently small, the handle problem is quickly solved. Discarded oak furniture will provide hardwood for blades. Cut a notch in the handle, fit the blade into it, and fasten with small nails or glue. The hardwood blades last longer, and when sanded to a smooth finish and painted with silver or aluminum paint, are convincingly realistic. (Daggers with sharp points are dangerous.) Thus, with a little paint and some pieces of old furniture, coupled with considerable ingenuity, Ali Baba's forty thieves can be armed without endangering either their lives or the budget.

Drink to me only with thine eyes. Goblets are a stage must. How could Macbeth's feast be set without goblets? Where does one find the goblets? Glass is impractical because actors are always sweeping them off tables in paroxyms of simulated rage or heaving them at ghosts in terror. Now the sweepable and heavable goblet is available in assorted sizes and styles. A small wood lathe and the butt ends of redwood four by fours, obtainable at any lumber yard for practically nothing, are all that is needed. It need not even be hollowed out, though to keep the actor from bumping his nose every time he pretends to drink, it would be well to cut a cone into the interior about one inch deep at its apex. This should allow even Cyrano's proboscis ample space. Paint the shallow inside bottom black to give it depth and the outside gold or silver, and you have a handsome drinking goblet with which to grace any stage table. Katherine can throw these at Petruchio for many performances without replacement.

GI Joe can find guns. Another baffling problem faced by property crews is providing the army with guns. Operas and musical comedies such as *Carmen* and *My Maryland* can make effective use of soldier choruses, but what is a soldier without a gun? Rifles of the flintlock or cap-and-ball vintage can usually be rented from costume houses, but economically this is unsound, since money spent on rentals does not build up the property department of any theatre. How, then, may guns be made or obtained? If those required are modern, they can occasionally be obtained from certain large surplus stores. At the beginning of World War II the army was forced to train with fake weapons. A dummy rifle was rushed into production and used in training camps. The bolt action works and at a little distance the gun is indistinguishable from the Springfield rifle of the World War I. Many of these practice rifles found their way into the hands of surplus army goods purchasers at the end of the war. Even these super salesmen have failed to create a demand for dummy rifles and they are usually eager to dispose of them at nominal prices.

The theatrical gunsmith. Older guns are not so easily procured. There are companies which specialize in the sale of old arms, but the prices are high. Again we must call upon ingenuity. First find a model, either genuine or a picture of the one you want to reproduce. Trace the outline of the stock and forward grip on a piece of soft white pine two inches thick, then cut out what you have traced on a band saw. Next, being careful to watch the direction of the grain, shape the stock with a draw knife and a wood rasp. The barrel can be made from an old broom stick or doweling and fitted to the stock. The role of trigger guard will be adequately filled by a pipe hanger; and the outside hammer, which usually distinguishes the old rifle, can be cut from ¼″ plywood and fastened in place by a small nail or screw. Other refinements may be added in proportion to the desired authenticity.

It would be possible to go on indefinitely devising methods of making or faking stage properties. It may be, however, more useful to draw some broad conclusions which naturally grow out of this discussion.

First, the necessity for economy is recognized by all who deal with the financing of college or community theatres. Budgets are small, and at the same time everyone would like to see the production presented in the most professional manner possible. How to bring these two factors into harmony is one of the theatre's most vexatious problems. Nevertheless, there is hope that it is not insoluble.

No substitute for ingenuity. Because there is almost always a solution, the next logical step is the selection of an ingenious individual as property manager. Ingenuity is often a matter of necessity, but the person charged with the procurement or creation of properties should also be an optimist. It is far easier to wring one's hands and mutter "impossible" than it is to scheme, devise, and think. Every problem has its solution, even though it may be a compromise. An eager, constructive approach to the production is of great importance, for as the work progresses, many difficulties solve themselves.

Materials for properties are found everywhere—in attics, surplus stores, junk heaps, and other strange places which are usually overlooked. The efficient property man observes automatically and catalogues mnemonically all information that may be ultimately useful. If his memory is good, he may recall information which will save hours of search and worry.

Finally, there is much to be said for the sheer fun and satisfaction which may be derived from the final appearance of a stage setting properly dressed. No matter how clever or artistic a setting may be, it is barren and cold without the appurtenances provided by the property crew. Those who engage in this work should take for their motto the boast of the Navy's Seabee battalions of World War II: "The difficult we do immediately; the impossible takes a little more time."

Add to that the virtuous comment, "I stayed within my budget" and you have the perfect property man.

The Business of Make-Up

Dr. George Osborne of the University of Utah School of Pharmacy became very interested in the small-scale manufacture of theatrical make-up materials, in addition to his interest in other phases of the theatre. Over a period of years he developed cosmetic formulas that anyone with reasonable skill and care could understand and compound. The formulas may be compared to a useful recipe book. Greater skills come with continued use of all recipes or formulas, but even a novice will soon find satisfaction in working with the formulas.

At a breakfast of a National Children's Theatre Conference, Dr. Osborne gave an impressive lecture-demonstration which proved to be one of the highlights of the entire convention. All guests received samples of cosmetics which were made before their eyes. Many theatre directors were amazed with the quality of the products and the simplicity of the processes. The following pages give for the first time the complete information prepared and compiled by Dr. Osborne as a special favor to the author and to educational theatre.

The Small-Scale Manufacture of Theatrical Cosmetics

The actor's face is covered with paint
To make him look like someone he ain't.

Theatrical make-up, as an item in the budget, is frequently the cause of considerable distress to the theatre manager. It is expensive. But the expense can be measurably cut down if there can be found someone, professionally qualified and interested in the theatre, who is willing to manufacture on a small scale the cosmetics necessary to stage performances.

The manager of the university theatre is fortunate if the university houses a college of pharmacy. These departments usually harbor someone whose interest in this direction can be aroused. The manager of the community or little theatre has a more difficult problem, but his best bet lies in his contact with a good pharmacist, creating and cultivating in him an interest in the cosmetic problems of the stage. Where there is interest there will be found ability.

Every pharmacist is a potential cosmetician: professionally his is the knack of putting together various ingredients with an aim toward elegance in the result. Since his formal training in pharmacy is broken up into units, he learns general rules of manufacture for particular types or classes of preparations. What he may not be aware of is that the large majority of the cosmetics used in the theatre lie perfectly within one or another of the types of pharmaceutical preparations with which he is already completely familiar. Given typical formulas, his problem becomes one of manipulation of those formulas to suit them to the needs of the group with which he is working.

By and large, the ingredients for the formulas given in this chapter are already on the pharmacist's shelves. Many of them are described in his official compendia, and if they are official, pharmacopoeial (U.S.P.) quality should be insisted upon.

Pigments such as yellow or golden ochre, raw or burnt umber, or ultramarine, are readily available from a paint manufacturer in a form sufficiently pure for most cosmetic uses. The pigments and dyes used in paste rouges are certified colors; if they cannot be purchased from local sources, they may be ordered from H. Kohnstamm & Co., Inc., 11–13 East Illinois Street, Chicago, Illinois. The following six shades or combinations of them will suffice for most purposes:

Light	Cosmetic Scarlet Lake	D. & C. Red #10
Medium	Cosmetic Medium Red Lake	D. & C. Red #11
Brilliant (Poppy)	Cosmetic Brilliant Red Lake	D. & C. Red # 9
Dark	Cosmetic Maroon Lake	D. & C. Red # 2
Orange	Bromo Acid	D. & C. Red #21
Strawberry	Cosmetic Geranium Lake	D. & C. Red # 3

While the perfumes used for street make-up are formulated from comparatively expensive components expressly to catch milady's fancy, those used in theatrical cosmetics are not all exotic. The smell of grease paint, often credited with elevating the pulse rate of even old troupers, arises from such simples as oil of rose (artificial, at that), witch hazel, and orange flower water. A special line of make-up perfumes is featured by Givaudan-Delawanna, Inc., and is available from their New York office, 330 West 42nd Street, New York 18, New York.

Cold creams. Creams in liquid or solid form exist in defiance of the adage that oil and water will not mix. They are not homogeneous systems, but rather suspensions of one of the phases in the other typical emulsions. The dispersion of the suspended phase is brought about and maintained by an agent called an emulsifier.

Cold creams themselves are solid water-in-oil emulsions, stiffened with beeswax, and emulsified with an alkali, usually borax. The original formula for cold cream is attributed to Galen (A. D., 131–201), who is also credited with, or accused of, fathering the profession of pharmacy. The variations of his formula are numerous, and there can be found in the literature on the market literally hundreds of cold creams, each different from the other.

Both theatrical cold cream and cosmetic cold cream are used chiefly to remove make-up; but the comparatively deep layer of grease paint on the skin of the actor requires an oilier product, one that will liquefy and penetrate more rapidly as it is applied, dissolving the greasy base, flushing away the pigments and dyes, and leaving the pores of the skin cleansed and open. When manipulating the proportions of the four major cold cream components, oil, water, borax, and beeswax, to formulate a cream with suitable characteristics, the following general considerations apply:

1. As the quantity of oil is increased in relation to the water, the cream will become stiffer rather than softer, as might be expected. If a maximum of 60 per cent of oil is exceeded, the cream will be unstable. A vegetable oil will require the addition of a preservative; methyl or propyl parahydroxybenzoate (methyl or propyl paraben) in strengths of 0.1 per cent to 0.2 per cent may be used. Mineral oil (heavy liquid petrolatum) obviates this precaution.

2. Water tends to soften the cream, which may, if the water ratio is too high, develop into a liquid product that is most unhandy for use in the dressing room. Generally speaking, the oil to water ratio may vary from 1:2 to 2:1. Our formulas (q. v.) approach the latter ratio.

3. As the proportion of wax increases, the cream becomes harder; paraffin and spermaceti will also contribute to the stiffness of the product.

4. Borax (sodium borate) should vary in amount from 5 per cent to 10 per cent of the beeswax. (The theoretical amount depends on the acid number of the wax.)

Oil-in-water systems are best emulsified when the phases are in the liquid state. The technique of manufacture of this type of preparation therefore, involves making two solutions of the components: the water-soluble ingredients are dissolved in the water, and the oil-soluble ingredients are dissolved in the oil. Both solutions are heated to the same temperature, usually about 160° F. (70° C.); they are mixed at this temperature; and the mixture is stirred until it congeals. When the cream reaches a temperature of 110° F. (45° C.), the perfume may be added without undue loss from evaporation. This procedure may be followed in the preparation of any of the formulas offered.

Theatrical Cold Cream, No. 1 (Hawkes and Osborne–Utah General I)

Mineral Oil	52.7 parts
Paraffin	6.8
Spermaceti	5.7
White Beeswax	9.1
Borax	1.4
Water	24.3
Perfume, *q.s.*	
To make	100.0 parts

Theatrical Cold Cream, No. 2 (Anderson and Osborne—Utah General II)

Mineral Oil	51.0 parts
Paraffin	6.6
Spermaceti	5.5
White Beeswax	12.1
Borax	1.1
Water	23.7
Perfume, *q.s.*	
To make	100.0 parts

Theatrical Cold Cream, No. 3 (P. R. B. III—Special Soft)

Note: This formula gives a very soft cream particularly suited to use in the cool night air for outdoor productions. It is not very stable and should be made up in small quantities.

Glycerin	1.0 parts
Sodium Borate	0.9
White Wax	14.1
Heavy Liquid Petrolatum	62.0
Distilled Water	13.0
Perfume, *q.s.*	
To make	100.0 parts

Theatrical Cold Cream, No. 4 (Lee and DeKay—Special Firm)

Note: Creams made from this formula were supplied to Purdue Play-shop and gave satisfactory service under routine theatre conditions.

Spermaceti	15.0 parts
White Wax	15.0
Liquid Petrolatum	48.0
Sodium Borate	1.0
Distilled Water	21.0
Oil of Rose, *q.s.*	
To make	100.0 parts

Grease paints. Grease paints, also called "bases" or "foundations," are suspensions of solid phases (pigments) in semisolid media (petroleum jelly); pharmaceutically they are ointments. Theatrically, the purpose of these paints is to cover the exposed skin of the actor and give him the complexion of the person he is representing on the stage. Then the features of the character are painted on with rouges, lining materials, and shading materials.

The solid phase, which constitutes about 50 per cent of the total weight of a grease paint, frequently contains covering agents and lubricants in addition to the pigments. Those in most general use include the following:

1. Titanium dioxide "covers" about fives times as well per unit area as does zinc oxide, but it is expensive. Therefore, combinations of these two chemicals are employed in a ratio of one part of titanium dioxide to two parts of zinc oxide as the covering agent.

2. Talc is the accepted lubricant; it should constitute 10 per cent to 12.5 per cent of the weight of the finished product or 20 per cent to 25 per cent of the weight of the total dry powders in the suspended phase.

3. The pigments are many and varied. They must be insoluble in water, and chemically, physically, and physiologically inert. Cosmetic lake colors and painters' pigments are useful in small quantities, as are the red and yellow oxides of iron. It is impossible to give definite proportions for pigment combinations that will yield reproducible results, because colors are not exactly standard. Every batch of red or yellow oxide of iron is different. Some are muddy and give a sallow color; others impart the desired red glow. To obtain the various shades the pigments and their amounts are varied. The pale pinks require less yellow and, indeed, less of all pigment. The ruddy male paint needs more red. Again, the individual pigments vary so much that any formula must be empirically adjusted to suit the batches available.

The semisolid suspending medium for the powdered portion of the products is made from white or yellow petroleum jelly (petrolatum or vaseline), stiffened with paraffin or softened with mineral oil as the conditions demand. The softer products are more easily applied and blended, and mixtures of mineral oil and petrolatum in proportions up to equal parts of each have been used successfully as a base for grease paints.

Perfume may be added without altering the basic formula. The least allergenic of the perfumes is rose oil.

A general formula for a grease paint may be given in terms of parts per hundred parts as:

Zinc Oxide-Titanium Dioxide, 2:1	25 to 30
Talc	10 to 12.5
Pigments	3 to 15
Heavy Liquid Petrolatum	20 to 25
Petrolatum	25 to 30
To make	100 parts

The general procedure involves mixing thoroughly the powdered ingredients, levigating the mixture to a smooth paste using the liquid petrolatum and part of the petroleum jelly as levigating agents, then taking up the paste in the remainder of the petroleum jelly. If an ointment mill is available, these products will improve greatly on milling. The lack of a mill requires more careful reduction of particle size by hand and more thorough mixing on the part of the manufacturer.

Grease paints are known by numbers which correspond to the shades. These numbers are arbitrarily assigned by manufacturers but, roughly, the shades darken as the numbers increase. A comparative color chart is given below; however, there is no restriction on shades and an interested cosmetician can "custom build" any shade desired.

Corparative Color Chart[1]
Grease Paint

Color	Miner's	Stein	Max Factor
White	1	22	15
Flesh	2	4	2½
Pink		1	2
Light Juvenile	4	2	1A
Dark Juvenile	5	5	
Juvenile		3	2A
Sunburn	6		3½
Dark Sunburn		8	7A
Indian	7	17	10
Cream	9	9	4½
Sallow	11	11	6
Olive	12	13	5A
Chinese	14	16	12

[1] Ivard Strauss, *Paint, Powder and Make-up,* (New York: Barnes & Noble, Inc., 1938), Supplement, Comparative Color Chart and Make-up Guide.

Color	Miner's	Stein	Max Factor
Hindu	15	20	9
Mulatto	16	14	11
Negro		19	17
Carmine	8	18	
Flesh Juvenile		4	3
Yellow		23	5
Suntan	13		6A

Poucher[2] lists a still different scale and gives formulas and instructions for preparing a few of his numbers. Tints up to and including his No. 3 are obtained by combining red and yellow pigment mixture in increasing amounts with the necessary white powders. The color of the pigment mixture should be a salmon pink that will look most natural in the bright lights of the stage. The following combination is recommended:

        Geranium Lake . . . . 15 parts
        Golden Ochre 85

This mixture can then be combined with the titanium dioxide zinc oxide talc combination as follows:

Number	Shade	Parts Pigment Mixture	Parts Total Whites
1	Very pale flesh (lady)	0.5	100
1½	Moderately pale	1.0	100
2	Fair complexion (youth)	2.0	100
2½	Medium flesh (young man)	5.0	100
3	Pale complexion (man 30–36)	8.0	100

When the shades in this table were tested in the laboratories of the University of Utah College of Pharmacy, it was observed that the paler shades were good, but the deeper ones were rather violently pink. To get a more satisfactory deep shade, the following combination was formulated:

        Geranium Lake . . . . 5 parts
        Golden Ochre 65
        Burnt Sienna 30

[2] William A. Poucher, *Perfumes, Cosmetics and Soaps*, (6th ed.; New York: Van Nostrand Company, Inc., 1950), III, 185 *et seq*.

The pigment mixture itself was of a bright yellowish cocoa hue. When the mixture was added to the titanium dioxide—zinc oxide—talc combination in the proportions suggested by Poucher in the table, the deeper shades were good, but the paler ones were not of much value. Ratios higher than 8 parts of pigment to 100 parts of total whites resulted in usable shades, rather "Latin" in character.

This work blasted a theory that was toyed with in the early work in the laboratory: that a single pigment mixture could be formulated from which the gamut of useful shades of grease paint could be run simply by combining the pigment with a greater or smaller quantity of whites. It now appears that no such standardization is possible and that, as a general rule, at least for "straight" grease paints, when the shades are made lighter, the pinks should be increased, and as they are made darker more browns should be used.

Poucher[3] proceeds up his scale,   recommending the addition of the following pigments to each 100 parts of dry (white) base:
No. 3½ (Slightly sunburnt) a brownish-red color for sunburnt effects:

Crimson Lake	2 parts
Golden Ochre	15
Burnt Sienna	1
To make	18

No. 4 (Dark flesh: sailor) is more yellow, and is tinted with:

Golden Ochre	5 parts
Armenian Bole	13
To make	18

No. 5 (Sallow: Chinese) is yellowish, and is obtained with:

Yellow Ochre	15 parts
Burnt Sienna	3
To make	18

No. 6 (Yellowish flesh: old man) is redder than No. 5, as follows:

Yellow Ochre	15 parts
Burnt Sienna	3
Geranium Lake	2
To make	20

[3] *Ibid.*

Formulas for other useful shades that have been formulated successfully here, are:

Juvenile (Simulating Stein No. 3, Factor No. 2A)

Titanium dioxide	9.50 parts
Zinc Oxide	19.00
Talc	11.50
Yellow Ochre	5.70
Red Oxide of Iron	0.65
Heavy Liquid Petrolatum	25.00
Yellow Petrolatum	25.05
Burnt Sienna	3.60
To make	100 parts

Elderly Man (Simulating Factor No. 5½)

Titanium Dioxide	9.50 parts
Zinc Oxide	20.00
Talc	12.00
Yellow Ochre	6.35
Red Ferric Oxide	0.85
Burnt Sienna	3.70
Liquid Petrolatum	23.70
Yellow Petrolatum	23.90
To make	100 parts

A slightly darker shade, also numbered 5½ was simulated as follows:

Titanium Dioxide	9.5 parts
Zinc Oxide	19.8
Talc	12.0
Yellow Ochre	6.5
Red Ferric Oxide	0.95
Burnt Sienna	3.75
Liquid Petrolatum	23.5
Yellow Petrolatum	24.0
To make	100 parts

Dark Sunburn (Simulating Stein No. 8, Factor No. 7A)

Titanium Dioxide	9.4 parts
Zinc Oxide	19.0
Talc	12.0
Yellow Ochre	5.5
Red Oxide of Iron	1.9
Heavy Liquid Petrolatum	23.8
Yellow Petrolatum	23.8
Burnt Sienna	4.6
To make	100 parts

Indian (Simulating Miner's No. 7, Stein No. 17, Factor No. 10)

Titanium Dioxide	9.4 parts
Zinc Oxide	19.0
Talc	11.8
Yellow Ochre	5.7
Red Oxide of Iron	2.4
Heavy Liquid Petrolatum	23.5
Yellow Petrolatum	23.5
Burnt Sienna	4.7
To make	100 parts

Male Hindu (Simulating Factor No. 8A)

Titanium Dioxide	4.0 parts
Zinc Oxide	8.0
Talc	8.0
Yellow Ochre	4.5
Red Oxide of Iron	4.3
Burnt Umber	6.8
Burnt Sienna	4.8
Heavy Liquid Petrolatum	19.2
Yellow Petrolatum	40.4
To make	100 parts

Liquid make-up. Products of this type fall easily into the pharmaceutical definition of lotions: suspensions of solid phases in liquid media. The suspended phase of liquid make-up is more copious than that of a lotion, but the principles of manufacture are the same. The commercial analogue of this type is the cosmetic stocking or liquid leg make-up. Theatrically, these preparations find their advantage in making up large skin areas, the torso, the legs, the arms.

The liquid most often used as the suspending medium for liquid make-up is a combination of propylene glycol, methyl cellulose mucilages, and water. Other diluents include alcohol and glycerin. Bentonite magma may be added as a suspending agent. Few generalities of formulation can be drawn: the rate of drying, the permanence of the pigment film, the equipment available to the manufacturer, the quantity of product to be prepared are all factors that may bring about variations in the typical formulas given here.

The pigmentation is the same for liquid make-up as it is for grease paints. The proportion of pigments to base is likewise the same: 50–50.

These preparations can be made in a mortar with a pestle; however, they are best manufactured with an electric mixer operating at a slow speed or in a "colloid mill." They should always be packaged with a warning to "shake well before using."

Liquid Base

Methyl Cellulose (4000 cps) 5%	60.0 parts
Alcohol	12.0
Sodium Benzoate	0.3
Glyceryl Monostearate	4.8
Glycerin	12.0
Propylene Glycol	12.0
Titanium Dioxide	24.0
Zinc Oxide	47.0
Talc	30.0
Yellow Ochre	10.5
Red Oxide of Iron	3.5
Burnt Sienna	8.2
Burnt Umber	4.0
Distilled Water	150.0

Note: If this formula seems too dry, an addition of 25 cc. of glycerin and propylene glycol may be made to each 500 cc. of base.

This base was used to make up the Negroes for *Show Boat* by varying it into three shades:

Light-dark Boy. Add 6 parts of burnt umber per 100 parts of base and dilute to the desired consistency with 5 per cent methyl cellulose.

Medium-dark Boy. Add 9 parts of burnt umber per 100 parts of base and dilute to the desired consistency with 5 per cent methyl cellulose.

Dark-dark Boy. Add 12 parts of burnt umber plus 14.3 parts of charcoal per 100 parts of base and dilute to the desired consistency with 5 per cent methyl cellulose.

Suntan Shades	*No. 1*	*No. 2*	*No. 3*	*No. 4*
Bentonite	3.	3.	3.	2.
Calamine	5.4	5.4	5.4	3.6
Titanium Dioxide	5.4	5.4	5.4	3.6
Propylene Glycol	5.	5.	5.	3.2
Burnt Umber	1.8	3.2	6.9	3.2
Red Ferric Oxide	.4	.4	.4	.3
Yellow Ochre	3.2	6.4	12.8	8.6
Rose Soluble	7.5	7.5	7.5	7.5

Water, a sufficient quantity,

To make 100 parts

The suntan shades numbered 1, 2, and 3, were formulated for the productions of *Carmen* and *The Great Waltz.* No. 4 was used for the Egyptians in *Antony and Cleopatra.*

Rouges. Rouges are of three general types: dry, cream, and paste. In the theatre paste rouges are preferred for ordinary purposes. Paste rouges resemble cerates in that they are ointment-like preparations stiffened with wax. Being made up in a greasy base, paste rouges blend easily with grease paints to give a natural "bloom" to the cheeks and lips of the straight character or to shade areas on other characters.

The pigments most frequently used in rouges are cosmetic lake colors. Some thirty-seven shades of red are certified by the Food and Drug Administration for use in drugs and cosmetics. However, combinations of the six common lake colors listed on page 175 will give a scale of red shades that will suit nearly every purpose. A good base for paste rouges is proposed in this formula:

Stearyl Alcohol	2.9	parts
Cocoa Butter	2.9	
White Beeswax	14.4	
Spermaceti	4.8	
Petrolatum	74.0	
Preservative	0.1	
Perfume	0.9	
To make	100.0	parts

The ingredients of this base should be melted together in a water-bath (or on low heat) and the pigments incorporated in the molten base. If large quantities of the base are made up, when small batches of rouge are desired, the requisite amount of base can be weighed out, softened, and worked up with the pigments.

The usual amount of pigment is a total of 8–10 parts per 100 parts of base.

Three representative formulas are given.

Pink Rouge (Haynie and Osborne No. 1)

Stearyl Alcohol	3.0	parts
Cocoa Butter	3.0	
White Beeswax	15.0	
Spermaceti	5.0	
Petrolatum	77.0	
D. & C. Red No. 3	8.0	
D. & C. Red No. 21	1.7	
Preservative	0.1	
Perfume	0.9	
To make	113.7	parts

Dark Red Rouge (Olds and Osborne No. 3)

White Beeswax	25.00	parts
Benzoinated Lard	10.00	
Petrolatum	62.29	
Aniline Violet	0.60	
D. & C. Red No. 11	8.00	
Perfume	1.00	
Preservative	0.01	
To make	106.90	parts

Red Rouge (Haynie and Osborne No. 2)

Stearyl Alcohol	3.0	parts
Cocoa Butter	3.0	
White Beeswax	15.0	
Spermaceti	5.0	
Petrolatum	77.0	
D. & C. Red No. 10	4.0	
D. & C. Red No. 11	4.0	
Preservative	0.1	
Perfume	0.9	
To make	$\overline{112.0}$	parts

Lining materials. These products are quite similar to dermatological pastes, since they are ointment-like preparations stiffened by the addition of dry powders. As the name implies, these materials are used to make lines or to draw features on the painted and rouged face; they may either trace features already there or create an entirely new set. They must be capable of retaining sharp definition on application, and they must also allow for blending without smearing or spreading. Here again the greasy base of these preparations facilitates their blending with each other and with the grease paint foundation.

Like grease paints, lining colors are designated by numbers arbitrarily assigned by different manufacturers. Below is a comparative color chart for these materials:

Comparative Color Chart[4]
Lining Colors

Color	Miner's	Stein	Max Factor
Black	13	17	1
Dark Brown	8	7	2
Light Brown	7	6	3
Dark Blue	3	10	4
Light Blue	2	8	5
Blue Gray	5	5	6
Blue Green	4	20	7

[4] Ivard Strauss, *Paint, Powder and Make-up*, (New York: Barnes & Noble, Inc., 1938), Supplement, Comparative Color Chart and Make-up Guide.

Color	Miner's	Stein	Max Factor
Green	9	19	10
Yellow	14	16	11
White	1	15	12
Purple Bronze		13	13
Bronze		14	14
Gray	6	3	15
Carmine	11	18	
Crimson	12	12	

Because of the nature of titanium dioxide and zinc oxide, the dry powders in the liners formulated herein must be either levigated before incorporation into the base, or the finished product must be milled to obtain a perfectly smooth product.

White Liner (Simulating Miner's No. 1, Stein No. 15, Factor No. 12)

Titanium Dioxide	10
Zinc Oxide	20
Talc	10
Starch	10
White Petrolatum	50
To make	100

Gray Liner (Simulating Miner's No. 5, Stein No. 5, Factor No. 6)

Titanium Dioxide	10
Zinc Oxide	12
Talc	10
Starch	10
Lamp Black	8
White Petrolatum	50
To make	100

Brown Liner (Simulating Factor No. 22)

Titanium Dioxide	2
Zinc Oxide	4
Red Ferric Oxide	6
Burnt Umber	6
Yellow Ochre	32
Yellow Petrolatum	50
To make	100

Eye shadows. These products are similar to lining materials, and indeed are frequently used interchangeably with them. Colors for use in eye shadows must be given special consideration because of the site of application. The Toilet Goods Association Board of Standards (Bulletin No. 232) makes the following general recommendations:

1. No coal-tar color of any kind should be used in preparations for use in the area of the eye. Colors which have been certified for cosmetics are not considered as certified for this type of preparation.
2. Carbon and Bone Black, as well as Oil Black, may be used in these preparations provided they are pure colors and do not contain harmful or deleterious impurities. . . .
3. Vegetable colors of known purity may be used in these preparations. Chlorophyll may be used, but specially prepared grades of chlorophyll containing copper should not be used.
4. Mineral and Earth colors of known purity may be used. . . .
5. Salts of cobalt may be used in these preparations only if they are insoluble salts and will not react with other ingredients of the preparation to form soluble cobalt compounds.

Thomssen[5] lists these formulas for eye shadows. They have been used successfully in theatrical work.

Eye Shadow Blue	White Beeswax	2.25
	Spermaceti	4.50
	Lanolin	4.50
	White Petrolatum	42.65
	Ultramarine	15.28
	Zinc Oxide	30.57
	Perfume	0.25
	To make	100.00
Eye Shadow Brown	Beeswax	2.25
	Spermaceti	4.50
	Lanolin	4.50
	White Petrolatum	41.35
	Zinc Oxide	26.90
	Burnt Umber	20.00
	Perfume	0.50
	To make	100.00

[5] E. G. Thomssen, *Modern Cosmetics*, (3rd ed.; New York: Drug and Cosmetic Industry, 1947), pp. 293–294.

Eye Shadow Green	White Beeswax	3.36
	Spermaceti	6.72
	Lanolin	6.72
	White Petrolatum	43.75
	Chrome Oxide	15.00
	Zinc Oxide	24.20
	Perfume	0.25
	To make	100.00

Powders. Cosmetic powders are simple mixtures of dry, powdered ingredients; pharmaceutical powders have one added qualification: they have medicinal properties. Face powders are designed to eliminate the shine that arises from the naturally oily condition of the skin and to give it a smooth appearance. In the dressing room, powder serves, in addition to removing the shine of the greasy paints, to "set" the make-up and to blend the lines by moderating their definition.

Because they are applied to a greasy surface, theatrical powders must be of the heavy type. Like grease paints, powders must cover, and this property is derived from titanium dioxide and zinc oxide. Talc provides "slip" or lubrication, making possible easy and smooth application of the powder to the exposed areas. It is necessary to make the powder sufficiently adhesive to "hold" under the usual treatment on stage; this requirement is supplied by calcium stearate, magnesium stearate, or zinc stearate. Finally, there should be a binder for the color and the perfume to facilitate the distribution of both through the batch during the manufacturing operation; calcium or magnesium carbonate is added for this purpose.

In the process of manufacture, tinting is achieved by preparing combinations of pigments and the carbonate and mixing these "colors" with the base. Theatrical powders frequently run darker than their cosmetic counterparts; these more intense shades can be achieved by increasing the ratio of color to white base. Theatrical powders can also be coarser than cosmetic face powders. (The French, so 'tis said, sift their cosmetic powders through fine silk panties!) After mixing the powders, the finished product should be passed through a fine sieve to reduce the particle size and "homogenize" the powder.

Powders, too, have been assigned numbers according to the following chart:

Comparative Color Chart[6]
Face Powders

Color	Miner's	Stein	Max Factor
White	1	1	1
Light Pink		2	2
Pink		3	3
Flesh	2	4	10B
Rachel	10	6	7R
Sunburnt	6	10	9
Cream	9	7	12
Lavender		17	14
Ruddy	6	23	4
Natural		18	6
Hindu	15	11	19
Peach	3	16	
Othello		13	20
Suntan	13	4	5
Sallow	11	9	

The powder base and the colors, formulas for which are given here, do not simulate commercially available theatrical powders. These few shades are adaptable to most cases; formulation of other shades is easy and the possibilities are unlimited.

White Base for Heavy Powders

Titanium Dioxide	3.00
Zinc Oxide	21.25
Talc	68.29
Zinc Stearate	4.17
Precipitated Chalk	2.25
Perfume	1.04

Note: Unless otherwise indicated, use 5 parts of coloring to 75 parts of this base.

Peach Coloring

Precipitated Chalk	59
Golden Ochre	40
D. & C. Red #3	1

[6] Ivard Strauss, *Paint, Powder and Make-up*, (New York: Barnes & Noble, Inc., 1938), Supplement, Comparative Color Chart and Make-up Guide.

Pale Rachel Coloring

    Precipitated Chalk 75
    Golden Ochre 25

Natural Coloring

    Precipitated Chalk 75
    Golden Ochre 24
    D. & C. Red #3   1

Suntan Coloring

    Precipitated Chalk 36
    Yellow Ochre 58
    D. & C. Red #3   6

Dark Suntan Coloring

    Precipitated Chalk 36
    Yellow Ochre 50
    D. & C. Red #3   6
    Burnt Umber   8

Note: Mix 50–50 with the white base above to obtain a very dark powder.

Hair whiting. Hair may be grayed by covering it with white or silver pigments, applied in either the dry or liquid state. Dry white powder (including corn starch) or powdered aluminum may be combed through the hair to add an appearance of dignity or age. Some actors prefer to use face powder of a pale shade for these purposes. Dry-powdering the hair, however, is not the most satisfactory method of applying hair whiting. It is messy and cannot stand "the fingernail test." The powder sifts out of the hair onto the costumes, requiring retouching of the make-up and frequent brushing of costumes. Liquid whiting is preferred.

Wet White (French White)

    Bismuth Subcarbonate 7.5
    Zinc Oxide 10.0
    Titanium Dioxide 2.5
    Glycerin 30.0
    Alcohol 10.0
    Orange Flower Water 40.0
                To make 100.0

Hair blacking. This preparation has been used for blacking hair for Indians; it also came in handy when an albino was cast as Tony in *They Knew What They Wanted.* It washes out easily and covers well.

Lamp Black	10
Olive Oil	90
To make	100

Spirit gum. This adjunct of the buskin and wig is as variously constituted as is the cream used to remove make-up from the face. In its simpler forms, spirit gum is one of the following: (1) solution of mastic in ether; (2) solution of mastic in alcohol; (3) solution of sandarac in ether; (4) solution of shellac in alcohol; (5) a combination of any of these gums in any of the solvents.

The gums are dissolved in a mixture of the solvents by allowing them to macerate for several days (or as long as three or four weeks). The product should then be clarified by straining it. The spirit gum that has been used at Utah contains:

Mastic	50
Acetone	10
Alcohol, a sufficient quantity,	
To make	100

The product is fairly slow-drying, since it was formulated for outdoor productions. A faster-drying preparation could be effected by using ether or by using this formula:

Mastic	3.7
Sandarac	7.4
Rosin	22.2
Ether	7.4
Alcohol	59.3
To make	100.0

Epilogue. After the cosmetician from the theatre group has become thoroughly acquainted with the standard formulas and with the rules of general formulation, he may wish to work with the manufacturing technicians in the laboratories and produce "custom" cosmetics for each show. To do this, he will take into account the actor, the part, the theatre, the costumes, and the lights. Thus he can achieve the ultimate in making up a show—a maximum of service at a minimum cost.

PART THREE

After the Show

XVI

BOOKKEEPING MADE EASY

The Ten Commandments for Bookkeepers and Business Staff

1. Thou shalt not mix up the theatre's silver and gold with thine own, for such a practice may cause an embarrassing problem of identification.

2. Remember to record all transactions before sundown of the day of their happening while they are still hot.

3. Honor thy state and federal tax collectors in those things which concern them, for they are a vengeful lot and their records extend even to the second generation.

4. Thou shalt pay all bills promptly in order to generate good will and beget a high credit rating; moreover, thou shalt thus gain cash discounts which may mean the margin of difference between success and failure.

5. Thou shalt have no more than one purchasing agent at one time, and all requests shall go through him and bear his personal signature.

6. Thou shalt beget a bookkeeping system which will give clearly all necessary information and not confuse the unlearned with needless detail. Remember that bookkeeping is a service and not a business per se.

7. Thou shalt not purchase nor allow others to purchase any unnecessary thing because it is cheap, for the theatre will not hold him guiltless who collects white elephants.

8. Thou shalt not bear false witness through outdated, misleading reports.

9. Thou shalt not permit any extravagant or prodigal department within the theatre to usurp another department's savings and economies.

10. Thou shalt follow religiously the established procedures of record-

ing income and expenses, for exceptions can lead to an ignominious downfall.

A Functional Bookkeeping System

Inefficient, careless bookkeeping is the cause of countless business failures. That theatres have been particularly inattentive to this phase of their art is a fact recorded in their premature obituaries. Such fatal mistakes as unwise and uncontrolled buying, outdated reports, lack of internal control over cash, inadequate fixing of responsibility, inaccurate entries, and plain old-fashioned carelessness have too often sounded the death knell.

There are two important functions of bookkeeping: (1) to facilitate business and (2) to keep a record.

Any adequate theatre bookkeeping system should provide for the following:

1. Financial information divided into five types:

a. Income

b. Costs

c. Budget

d. Information required by the institution or state or federal government.

e. Special types of information helpful to management.

2. An accurate, current, running account of budgetary balances for each item.

3. Control over buying and spending.

4. Flexibility and simplicity of operation.

Financial information may vary considerably according to both the theatre management and governmental and institutional requirements. In general, the basic objective of any theatre bookkeeping system should be to provide current, up-to-date reports regarding income and costs. The type of information needed must be determined by its usefulness to the theatre and by what is legally required.

Accurate running of budgetary balances can be accomplished by setting up combination budget and cost accounts in a ledger. Under this method, an account is set up for each budget item such as scenery, lights, costumes, rentals, advertising, tickets, etc., and each of these accounts is credited with the specific amount of its budget. For instance, scenery may be credited with $500, properties with $150, and so on. Commitments and/or expenditures are then charged against each appropriate credit. Because many theatres are not underwritten by outside funds, budgeted costs must be set up entirely on the basis of anticipated revenues. The bookkeeping system should show accurate and current data comparing expected and actual revenues on one side and expected and actual costs on the other side.

Controls over income and expenditures must be well understood and fully accepted by all concerned. Although the bookkeeping system cannot compel internal control, it can give information which will enable the management to establish and enforce necessary controls.

Flexibility and simplicity of operation are most desirable. Flexibility means adaptation of fundamental principles to a given situation. There must be a balance between being too rigid and too lax. Simplicity means doing that which has to be done with a minimum of confusion and with as few operations as possible.

Bookkeeping Tools

1. Requisitions
2. Purchase orders
3. Invoices
4. Checks or vouchers
5. Ledgers
6. A good filing system

1. The requisition is a request for materials or services, usually instigated by the manager of the theatre. It is routed from the theatre to a central purchasing authority who prepares the purchase order (Fig. 30).
2. The purchase order is an order for materials or services and is usually prepared from a requisition. It is issued by the purchasing authority or his authorized representative to the business house or vendor (Fig. 31).
3. The invoice is an itemized list of materials or services. When a supplier's invoice is approved by the proper authority, it represents an amount payable. Many people do not know the difference between a statement and an invoice. A statement merely says that you owe so much and does not as a rule list the items as does the invoice. Most firms do not pay statements; they pay only invoices.
4. The voucher is a serially numbered order to pay one or more invoices. Checks are issued in payment of vouchers. A combination voucher-check may be used for expenditures. One way to do this is to have two or more copies of the voucher-check. The original copy, signed by the disbursing officer, represents the check portion. The copy represents the

REQUISITION

(Two Copies to Purchasing Department)

Date_____ 19___

No._____

Order
No. _____

Please Furnish the Following Items Not Later Than _____

Charge To _____

Deliver To:

Account
No. _____

Item No.	Quantity	Description	Estimated Cost	Actual Cost
1				
2				
3				
4				
5				
6				
7				
8				

Quotations May Be Obtained From:

Head of Department

Purchasing Agent

FIG. 30.

PURCHASE ORDER
Fireball Theatre
Purchasing Department

Purchase
Order No.

_____
(Name of Firm Furnishing

_____
Requested Materials)

_____

Ship the following Merchandise:

Quantity	Description	Price

1. Invoices must be rendered in triplicate and sent to the Purchasing Department.
2. Place Purchase Order Number on all invoices, packages and correspondence.
3. Bills of Lading must accompany the invoices of all freight shipments.
4. Acknowledge receipt of this order giving cost and date of shipment.

FIG. 31.

voucher portion and bears the same serial number as the check. The copy with the invoices attached is then filed in numerical sequence.

5. The ledger is a book of accounts. An account is a classified item of asset, liability, expense, income, or equity. Each control account may have several subsidiary accounts or subdivisions. In the case of our sample theatre bookkeeping system, the principal accounts are the "Plays." Each play is broken down by budget object. Each budget object is further broken down to classify expenditures by materials and labor.

6. A good filing system is one in which something can be found readily when it is wanted; it is not just a place to put things. A system which is adequate for purposes of information can be set up in two sections:

  a. An alphabetical file of the sellers of merchandise who have orders outstanding.

  b. A file of paid orders by budget object, e.g., scenery, costumes, etc. However, for audit purposes it is advisable to have copies of invoices attached to numerically filed vouchers. Both methods of filing can be used for convenience and accuracy.

General Bookkeeping Procedures

Bookkeeping procedures follow in general the same overall pattern. Expenses are charged on the left hand side of the ledger, (Dr), and income is credited on the right hand side, (Cr). The excess of accumulated credits (Cr) over debits (Dr) represents a gain, profit, or net income. Excess debits (Dr) over credits (Cr) represents excess expenditures over income, or a loss (Fig. 35, Page 204).

In processing expenditures through the bookkeeping system, procedures flow from the requisition, to the purchase order, to the invoice, and finally through the paid voucher.

If a simple expenditure record were maintained, the requisition and purchase order would be ignored when recording. The check, in payment of the invoice, would represent the posting medium to the account. The account would appear somewhat as follows:

Scenery Expense Dr   **A/C No. 1**

Check. No.	Description	Amount Dr		Cum. Total	
152	B + B Supply Company - Lumber	151	16	151	16
165	B + B Supply Company - Hardware	115	25	266	41

FIG. 32.

In case the order were to be recorded, the requisition and/or purchase order would be posted to the account as an (order outstanding) encumbrance (Enc). The account would then appear on this order:

Scenery Expense Dr   A/C No. 1

P.O. No.	Ck. No.	Description	Enc (cane)		Amount Paid Dr		Cum. Total	
101	✓	B+ B Supply Co.-Lumber	160	00			160	00
102	✓	B+ B Supply Co.-Hardware	105	00			265	00
101	152	Paid in full	(160	00)	151	16	256	00
102	165	Paid in full	(105	00)	115	25	266	41

FIG. 33.

When operating on a budget, the account would be extended one step further: A column showing the budget balance for each item is charged against the account.

Scenery Expense Dr   A/C No. 1

P.O. No.	Ck. No.	Description	Enc (cane)		Amount Paid Dr		Labor Dr		Budget Balance	
✓	✓	Budget							500	00
101	✓	B+B Supply Co.	160	00					340	00
102	✓	B+B Supply Co.	105	00					235	00
101	152	Paid in full	(160	00)	151	16			243	84
102	165	Paid in full	(105	00)	115	25			233	59
✓	170	Payroll					115	00	118	59

FIG. 34.

Reports are made from accounts. From the above account, the report could show the original budget of $500.00, less expenditures of $381.41, leaving a budget saving of $118.59. The same type of information could be shown for all other expense accounts.

A Sample Bookkeeping System

A well-known state university has a theatre operated through the university administration. At the beginning of each school year an allocation is made from student fees to the university theatre. This allocation, or apportionment, is to cover student admissions to the plays during the year. Actually, it amounts to the sale of a large number of student and faculty theatre tickets at a discount.

After season-ticket sales, each play must take in enough cash from

FIG. 35.

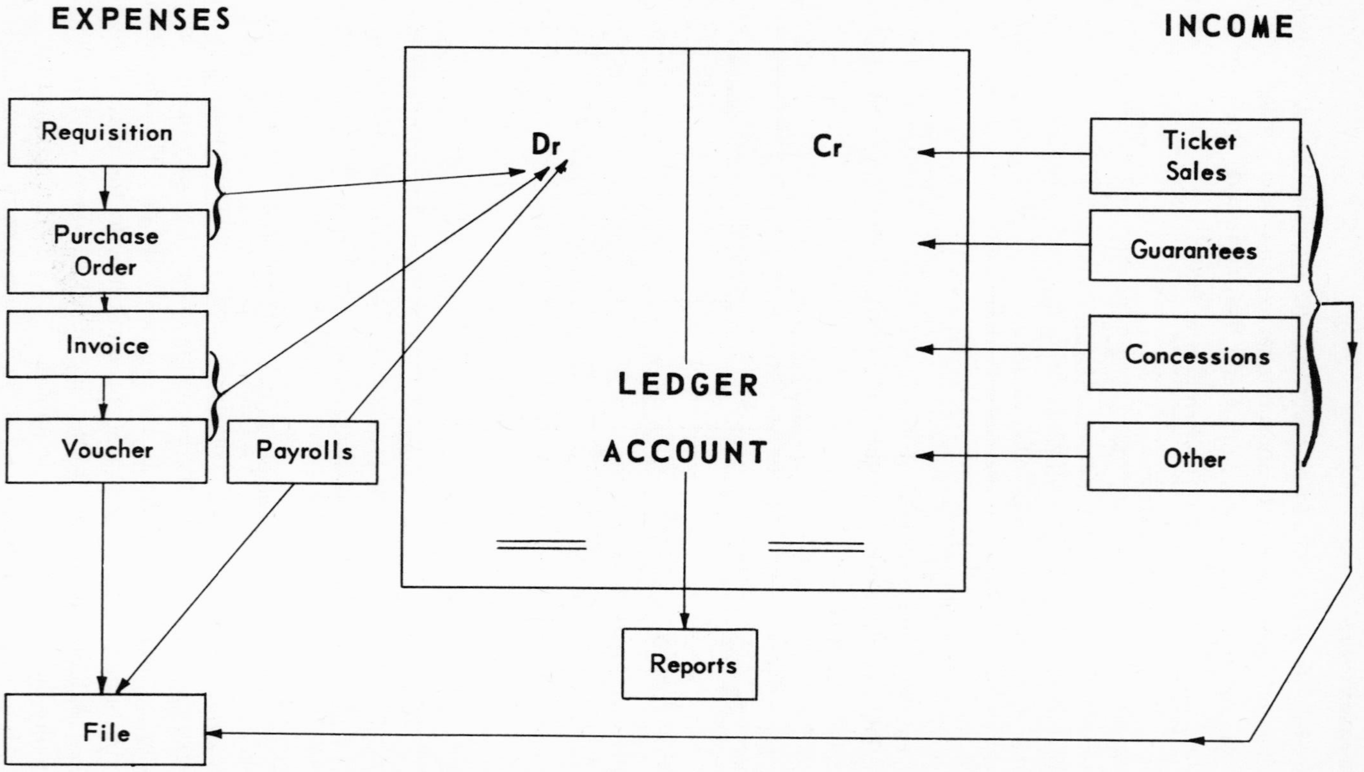

INCOME

Ticket Sales

Guarantees

Concessions

Other

Cr

LEDGER ACCOUNT

Dr

Reports

Payrolls

EXPENSES

Requisition

Purchase Order

Invoice

Voucher

File

single-play sales to meet expenditures not covered by its share of season sales and apportionment.

Accounts are set up so that financial reporting can be done by productions. Each play has a separate budget. Operating accounts are maintained to show running budget balances in addition to encumbrances and expenditures. Allocations from apportionment and season ticket sales are credited to each play as soon as the final figures are in. In addition to breakdowns by completed plays, reports are prepared to show the amount of cash needed in order to meet scheduled expenditures of future shows.

Accounting for purchases. Purchasing is done through the university purchasing department upon requisition from the theatre manager. Pre-numbered requisitions are prepared by the theatre manager's office in triplicate. The original is forwarded to the purchasing department for a purchase order. The duplicate is placed in a vendor's file and the triplicate is retained by the bookkeeper for posting to the ledger.

The requisition carries the following five points of information:

> Name and address of supplier.
> Number and name of items wanted.
> Price per item (quotations) and total amount.
> Play and budget object to be charged.
> Delivery or pickup instructions.

Sometimes it is necessary to obtain materials or services immediately. A working agreement usually exists between the purchasing agent and the theatre manager for these emergencies. This agreement allows for the manager of the theatre to call in his order direct to the supplier. In such cases, the purchase order number assigned to this order is obtained by telephone from the purchasing department, and is called in to the supplier with the order. The requisition is then made out as usual, except that the purchase order number is added as a part of the requisition. The purchase order then is sent to the supplier as a confirmation of the verbal order by the theatre manager.

The pre-numbered purchase order shows all the information as shown on the requisition, and in addition lists billing instructions to the supplier. It is prepared in four copies. The original is sent to the supplier. The duplicate goes to the university financial officer, the triplicate to the theatre manager, and the quadruplicate is retained for the file. The theatre manager attaches his copy of the purchase order to his copy of the requisition and replaces both back in the vendor file to await arrival of the supplier's invoice.

Invoices are submitted in triplicate by the supplier to the purchasing department, where they are immediately routed to the theatre manager for approval. Upon receipt of the invoice, the theatre manager pulls the purchase order from the vendor file, checks the invoice for completeness, and determines whether the materials or services have been received. This is done by securing signatures on the invoice of the person actually receiving the materials or services. The invoice is then approved for payment, signified by the theatre manager's signature on the invoice.

Two copies of the approved invoice are then returned to the purchasing department to be passed for payment. The triplicate copy of the invoice is attached to the purchase order, the purchase order is stamped "CANCELLED," and the completed order is passed to the bookkeeper for posting to the ledger.

Payrolls. Complete payroll records are kept by the university payroll department. However, information necessary for cost purposes is kept by the theatre. This is accomplished by means of individual time cards, prepared in triplicate. Data shown include, in addition to time worked, rate and gross pay, the budget object, and play to be charged. The original and duplicate time cards are given to the bookkeeper, who prepares a payroll schedule and recapitulation from the time cards, and posts the totals to the proper budget object under the proper play from the payroll recapitulation. This may seem somewhat elaborate, but it actually avoids duplication of payment, omission of payment, and any confusion as to amount.

Accounting for income. Income of the theatre comes from the following sources:

Student apportionment
Season-ticket sales
Single-play sales
Gifts
Guarantees
Program advertising and miscellaneous
Concessions

Cash from season-ticket sales is credited to a temporary income account until the season-ticket sale is over. After the season sale audit has been completed and the box-office report made out, season-ticket sales are divided equally among all plays, and each play is credited with its share of season-ticket income. Each play is also credited with an equal share of student apportionment income.

Cash from single-play sales is credited directly to that play, as are guarantees from traveling shows, and other items which can be identified with the play.

Advertising space in the programs is let out on a contract basis for the season, and programs for each play carry the same advertising. If for any reason extra program advertising is sold for one play only, such extra revenue should be so credited. Program advertising income is treated in the same way as season-ticket sales and student apportionment.

Reports. Some reports are prepared for the theatre management to show comparisons between budgeted expenditures and actual expenditures for completed plays:

UNIVERSITY THEATRE
BUDGET REPORT

Name of Play	Budget	Total Expenditures	(Over) Under Budget
Tom Sawyer	$2269.66	$2699.69	($430.03)
Titian	2294.66	1996.04	298.62
Magic Rose and the Ring	2244.64	1816.19	428.45
Totals	$6808.96	$6511.92	$297.04

The above report would indicate that a saving has been effected on budgeted expenditures of completed plays of $297.04. This could mean that more efficient operations have been placed into effect than planned on, or it could mean that the budget was too high for these particular shows in the first place. At any rate, the saving can be applied against unforeseen expenditures of future shows.

Single-play reports are made from the accounts to show income by source and expenditures by budget for completed plays: (Fig. 36)

UNIVERSITY THEATRE

SINGLE PLAY REPORT

TITIAN

(One of the four plays comprising the season)

Income:

  Ticket Sales:

    Share of Season Sales:

1/4 of $5174.00	$1293.50		
Less Sales Tax........	25.87		
Net Season Sales		$1267.63	
Single Play Sales:			
Gross Single Sales	187.50		
Less Sales Tax........	3.75		
Net Single Sales...........		183.75	
Total Ticket Sales			$1451.38

  Guarantees:

Ogden....................	250.00	
Kaysville.................	150.00	
Total Guarantees..............		400.00

  Concessions Income 25.75

               Total Income...... $1877.13

Expenses:

Scenery......................	51.14
Properties.....................	7.50
Makeup	4.12
Costumes	155.55
Miscellaneous	25.61
Royalties	40.00
Programs......................	95.28
Ushers........................	50.00
Electrician....................	15.75
Sound Operator.................	16.20
Janitorial	37.95
Hall Rentals...................	90.00
Scripts.......................	9.70
Tickets.......................	22.58
Advertising and Publicity	140.25
Meals, Lodgings, Travel	112.50
Salaries......................	844.13

          Total Expenses.... $1718.26

          NET INCOME ....$ 158.87

FIG. 36.

Another type of report is prepared to show the amount of cash needed to meet scheduled expenditures from future shows:

UNIVERSITY THEATRE
SCHEDULE OF CASH NEEDED TO
MEET SCHEDULED EXPENDITURES

Net Income From Operations to Date		$1,000.02
Less Unexpected Budgets of Future Shows:		
Patchwork Girl	$2,126.00	
The Old Maid	1,035.08	3,161.08
Cash needed to meet scheduled expenditures		($2,161.06)

XVII

HOW TO KEEP INTERESTING AND USEFUL RECORDS

When the director and manager look at the coming season beset with its insomnia-producing questions, they realize that the end of one season is always the beginning of the next. As they gaze into the crystal ball, they see no answers, only questions, questions:

What plays shall we present next year?

What plays have we done in the last five years?

Which were most successful?

How can we improve over the past season?

What suggestions have we picked up from the patrons?

What results did we get from the newspapers?

Do we have samples of the stories and advertisements we ran?

How much business did we get from our mail orders?

Is our mailing list up to date?

How many of those handbills did we print?

How much did they cost?

Do we have samples of our brochures of last year?

When should we launch our campaign for next season?

Psychologists tell us that to ease the pressure and worry we must take concrete steps to do something immediately; there must be positive action rather than negative. In thinking of theatre problems constructively, it is often advantageous to look backward before looking forward. The most tranquilizing first aid would be a record and a file.

A theatre without a record is like a clock without hands: it keeps going, but it tells you nothing, and it measures nothing. And a poor record consisting of incomplete and inaccurate information is almost as useless as none at all. A well-planned file, which neither accumulates needless and burdensome details nor omits items of importance, is a source of constant guidance to every progressive organization whether it be business, church, school, or theatre.

How does one define a good record? It is a collection of well-arranged information for immediate as well as for later use. It is a clear, complete, and accurate account of what happened and how it happened. It is not a miscellaneous batch of clippings in a big envelope; it is not busy work; it need not be expensive. Excellent scrapbooks have been compiled on sheets of paper 8½″ × 11″ or larger. Properly arranged these sheets can be permanently bound at a book bindery. This makes a most helpful book. Some theatres buy a large scrap book and paste into it.

How does one keep a file? A useful file is kept up to date as the events progress when the material is fresh and clear. Any attempt to catch up on even a few days' backlog makes the business of filing a burden rather than pleasure. It should be arranged in a convenient order so that it is easy to follow. It may be arranged alphabetically, topically, or chronologically. The kind of organization used should suit the theatre's needs. All notes accompanying the clippings or samples should be complete and self-explanatory. To forget to fill in the details promptly is to forget them almost entirely. Need one say that the file should never require a personal interpreter to explain the details? It often happens that a file is perfectly clear to the one who compiled and kept it but not to anyone else. For example, a zoology department of a large university had a curator who decided that it would be easier to catalogue all the specimens in the laboratory by number. Each number would correspond with a number in his book where the full information was contained. If, for example, one saw an earthworm in a bottle with Number 13 on it, he could then go to the curator and get the full scientific data on the worm. This method had one great advantage as far as the curator was concerned—it made him as nearly indispensable as a man could possibly be. The keys were his. He liked the system and he had no wish to change it, for it gave him a feeling of security such as few professors ever know. The situation, however, became so increasingly awkward that one day his superiors decided to fire him and change the system. They planned to attach the information about each specimen right on the mounting or container—standard practice in most laboratories. The climax to the little drama came when the head of the department said to the curator: "We have decided to release you as of now. You will receive two weeks' severance pay. We now request that you turn your record book of the collection to us."

The curtain line was spoken softly but firmly: "I appreciate the two weeks' severance pay, but I am sorry to tell you that the record book has been lost, and I cannot find it."

It is well to have the theatre record arranged in two parts:

1. *A standard letter-size file case* ($8\frac{1}{2}'' \times 11''$) is most commonly used, but the larger legal size may be preferred. Materials can be placed in labeled folders and arranged for handy reference. In this file case there will be such items as audience surveys, correspondence, pictures, portraits, printed programs (a few copies of each), recording tapes and phonograph records, and posters which are not too large. Mailing lists are usually but not always kept in $3'' \times 5''$ files.

2. *The scrapbook* is invaluable as a reservoir of information. This book should encompass a complete theatre year, usually from autumn to spring. Such a unit is easy to handle and convenient for reference. There are a few things in the scrap book which should be repeated every year.

a. *A chart showing the principal names of officials behind the theatre plus the constitution and by-Laws* should preface every annual because the names change and the constitution and by-laws may also change. If this part of the record is more than a year old, it will probably contain errors. Figure 37 is an illustration of a theatre organization: (A constitution and by-laws appear in the appendix.)

The constitution and by-laws should not only keep the objectives before the officers, but they should serve to expedite and facilitate operations. If the organization gets weighted down with parliamentary procedure and if the rules get in the way, it is better to set them aside entirely and conduct affairs on an informal basis.

b. *A summary of the minutes* of the year's meetings should be included. It is not necessary to have them complete, but it might be helpful to have the main items of business summarized.

c. *Clippings of all newspaper stories* should be neatly pasted in the scrapbook with dates, names, and other helpful comments written in the margins. It may be helpful to know that the season's first announcement had a prominent position on the page. If the theatre receives a full-

THE THEATRE ORGANIZATION
Fire Ball Theatre of Las Vegas

BOARD OF DIRECTORS
(OR COUNCIL OR PRODUCER)

George Allen
(President)

Brian Marchant
(Vice-President)

Marilyn Gregg
(Secretary)

Edith Goldwater
(Treasurer)

(and seven board members)

STAFF

Herbert Strike
(Director)

⟵⟶ *Lines of* ⟵⟶
Communication

F. S. Fisher
(Manager)

I. M. Helper
(Assistant Director)

O. C. Gallo
(Publicity)

Grace De Mille
(Designer)

Royal C. Penny
(Box Office)

Rhoda Cheval
(Costumer)

Gus Quick
(Property Man)

I. B. Rideout
(House Manager)

V. G. Watts
(Electrician)

Agnes Harper
(Bookkeeper)

Ned Paulos
(Stage Manager)

FIG. 37.

page spread, which is possible if plans are laid well in advance, the paper can be folded neatly in four, and the technique of how the page was obtained can be explained. The formula or recipe for obtaining such publicity should be kept—it might work again. Besides having a copy of a page spread in the scrapbook, it is important to have several extra copies in the big file. Sometimes it is even wise to have the newspaper run off a hundred or more extras for publicity uses. If this is requested in advance, it is a simple matter; if extra pages are not requested for several days after the run, it may be impossible to obtain them. The more carefully and completely this important work is recorded, the more valuable the book will be. One word of caution: Don't let people borrow the scrapbook or get into it with a pair of scissors, or it will soon be a book of scraps. If someone really needs a copy of an article as it appeared in the paper, there are inexpensive ways of photographing it. The very name "scrapbook" seems to suggest scissors and pillage to some people.

d. *Copies of newspaper advertisements,* especially the effective ones, can be helpful in several ways. Setting up information as to what and how is time consuming if one has to start from scratch. The more exact and complete the layout, the better the final copy will be. When one has the advertisement as it finally appears, he can ask the printer to label the following on the margin for the record: Sizes and styles of types used, kind of border, size of space, and cost of the advertisement, which is, of course, based on the cost per column inch. For example, if the rate were $5 a column inch and you had an advertisement two columns wide and four inches deep, this would be eight column inches and cost $40. It might be a good idea to ask a printer how he would improve the advertisement so you could pass that on for the next time. It is smart to make use of the services of an expert whenever possible.

e. *Samples of brochures, handbills, and circulars,* should be accompanied with details showing how many were printed, who printed them, how much they cost, how they were distributed, and the estimated results. A simple illustration will clarify the points to be covered: A university theatre had a contractural arrangement with the student association to admit all students to the theatre for a reserved seat ticket on the presentation of a coupon from his handbook. For some reason, the students had shown little interest in picking up their free tickets. So the little circular which follows was designed and distributed to arouse interest. The attached notes describe it.

Your coupon
No. 7

is good for a reserved seat
ticket to the

PETRIFIED
FOREST

to be presented February 1, 2, 3 and 4.

....

TO SERVE YOU . . .
**Beginning Thursday, January 27, the Kingsbury Hall
Box Office will be open daily, 9 A.M. to 4 P.M.**

....

Exchange Coupon No. 7 for your FREE Ticket. Extra Tickets, $1.20, Tax Inc.

....

FIG. 38.   *Size:* 6″ x 9″ (a good size)   *Quantity:* 3,000

Stock: Inexpensive variety colored paper (pink, white, gray, red, blue)

Cost: Total $23.00 (including cut)   *Date:* Jan. 27

Results: By 10 a.m., there was a line at the box office and they kept coming. The idea is recommended for once or twice a year when things get dull. Avoid its overuse.

Distribution: Twenty-four alert and smiling students were assigned to the main entrances of all classroom buildings at 7:45 a.m. just three days before the show opened to pass out these handbills. It may have helped a little that women were assigned to the law, medical, and engineering buildings, while men were assigned to the nursing and home economics buildings. As the students came in, each received a handbill and a smile. The assignment took just 15 minutes.

f. *For instances on short sales speeches and announcements* should be kept in the scrapbook. A good example will save much time and make for a better speech. Improvements, refinements, and changes come easier when one has a pattern to follow. Speech samples are particularly hard to get because the talks are often given from notes and are seldom written out. However, it will help to write out some short speeches carefully as a preparation step. By the time they are written, they will be practically memorized.

The following two-minute talk proved successful, and the high school did not object to a brief interruption of English classes. If these talks are made by college people, the high school students will accept them more enthusiastically than if made by a teacher whom they may suspect as one trying to load them up. The same kind of announcement will be acceptable to college students.

Two-minute speech by a college student urging high school students to attend a University Theatre Production of *Romeo and Juliet.*

I hope that my comments can make the production of *Romeo and Juliet* more interesting and worthwhile to you when you see it next Friday afternoon in the University Theatre.

You already know that Shakespeare's tragedy, *Romeo and Juliet,* is by far the most famous love story of all literature. The author has woven the elements of drama, tragedy, and love with such skill as no other artist has even approached. You should know that Romeo Montague and Juliet Capulet come from opposing families who have intense hatred for each other. They are not just enemies; they are deadly enemies. Romeo's life would be in grave danger if he were recognized on the premises of Juliet's family. That is why the best known line of the play is so tragic. When Juliet says, "Romeo, Romeo, wherefore art thou Romeo," she means that she cannot understand how it could happen that the very name of the only person she loves is the name of a deadly enemy to her family. It seems strange that their love in no way checks the family hatred. It rages on until it finally brings a tragic death to both Romeo and Juliet.

As the play moves swiftly on, you keep hoping that something will happen to stop the terrible feud between the two families. The conflicts will hold you in suspense every minute.

The University Theatre costuming, scenery, and lighting for the show are magnificent. The cast is thoroughly prepared. They have been rehearsing intensely for several months. Every role is well cast. We are especially well pleased with our beautiful and talented Juliet, and also with Romeo who looks and acts the part which you would expect. You'll agree fully when you see the show. The more you know about the play, the more you will enjoy it. I hope that I have added something to your pleasure. Thank you.

g. *Television and radio announcements* are usually written out or put on tape. The necessary copies for the file can easily be obtained with a little persistence. These can be kept in the scrapbook and the big file. The scrapbook should make a cross reference to such information. When the publicity man can say, "This is what we did last time," he is beginning to set up a precedent of value.

h. *A brief summary of the record of ticket sales* can be a guide to progress. "I wonder how the sale compares with that of last year" is what the manager often wants to know. If the box office manager says, "Well, it looks good to me but I don't know how it stands with a comparable date of last year," he is not much help. It may be about half what it was last year and still look good to him. Trusting to the fates instead of to the facts is dangerous. If the box office has the day-by-day records of what happened in previous years, the manager can tell whether he had better put on the heat or relax. He must have such information in time to do something. "Security is mortals' chiefest enemy," says the witch in *Macbeth*. A notation of the weather with the ticket report will also be helpful.

i. *Samples of the tickets* used during the year may avoid confusion on a new order. A record of the kind, quality, and colors shown in the scrapbook will end any arguments on the subject. It is surprising to learn how hard it is to get hold of old tickets once the shows are over. To be sure one does not want old tickets lying around, but one sample of each group is important.

j. *A copy of every printed program* should be pasted in the scrapbook and a number of extras should go in the big file. One of the most annoying nuisance calls is for old playbills or programs, especially anniversary playbills, or those which have considerable information on the theatre or its people. Never, never lend the last copy of a printed program, for it won't come back. If you have any doubt, ask any manager of experience.

k. *Photographs and portraits* are valuable property, but one can hardly put them in a scrapbook. However, the book should have a list of them and a cross reference to the big file. It has happened countless times that a sudden call is made for a picture which could mean an excellent story for the theatre. The common remark, "We once had a picture of him but

I don't know where it went," is usually answered with the words, "That's sure too bad."

l. *Biographical information on the players* is naturally associated with photographs. In fact, some theatres attach a little picture in the upper right-hand corner of the "Actor's Biography." A suggested biography appears on the opposite page.

m. *It is provident to keep a sample of all successful publicity contests in the file.* If they are not too long, they could be pasted in the scrapbook. Good contest ideas are rare. A lively one will develop when the probable contestants know the answers to some of the questions offhand.

One quiz contest on *Julius Caesar* was successful in a college newspaper. There were thirty-seven entries and the idea stirred up considerable discussion and interest. It might work just as well in a city paper if the publisher would give it publicity and space while the theatre furnished the prizes. If the space has to be paid for at the regular advertising rates, the results might not be worth the cost.

For the contest which follows, the first prize award was a school yearbook valued at five dollars. The winner answered nineteen of the twenty questions correctly.

Literary Quiz on *Julius Caesar*
(Copy of first place winner)

1. Q. Give the name of Caesar's wife.
   A. Calpurnia.
2. Q. Who speaks the line, "Give up the ghost?"
   A. Cassius says, "Their shadows seem a canopy most fatal, under which our army lies, ready to give up the ghost."   (Act V, Scene I)
3. Q. Who says, "It was Greek to me"?
   A. Casca, a conspirator says this concerning the speech of Cicero.
                                                                (Act I, Scene II)
4. Q. Who says, "Cowards die many times before their death; the valiant never taste of death but once"?
   A. Julius Caesar says this before going to the Senate House.
                                                                (Act II, Scene II)
5. Q. What was the name of Shakespeare's Elizabethan theatre?
   A. The Globe Theatre.
6. Q. Who was the Roman emperor just before Julius Caesar?
   A. Pompey was the imperator just before Julius Caesar. Actually Augustus, heir of Caesar, was the first emperor in name.
7. Q. Name the Triumvirs of Julius Caesar.
   A. Octavius Caesar, Marcus Antonius, and Marcus Aemilius Lepidus.

ACTOR'S BIOGRAPHY

Name _____

Address _____

Telephone _____ Married or Single _____

(Picture)

Previous plays with name of the part played at this theatre:

_____

_____

_____

_____

_____

Any other plays and parts with other groups:

_____

_____

_____

_____

_____

Any accomplishments which would be of interest to our audience:

_____

_____

FIG. 39.

8. Q. Name the eight conspirators against Julius Caesar.
   A. Marcus Brutus, Cassius, Casca, Trebonius, Caius Ligarius, Decius Brutus, Metellus Cimber, and Cinna.
9. Q. Give the name of the character in *Julius Caesar* who warned Caesar of the impending tragedy.
   A. A soothsayer warned Caesar when he said, "Beware the ides of March."
   (Act I, Scene II)
10. Q. Who says, "Friends, Romans, countrymen, lend me your ears"?
    A. Marcus Antonius says this in his famous oration.
    (Act III, Scene II)
11. Q. Which of the seven wonders of the world is mentioned in a famous simile of the play?
    A. The Colossus of Rhodes. ". . . he doth bestride the narrow world like a Colossus."   (Act I, Scene II)
12. Q. Name the famous river mentioned in *Julius Caesar*.
    A. The Tiber River.   (Act I, Scene II)
13. Q. Who says, "My heart doth joy that yet in all my life I found no man but he was true to me"?
    A. Brutus says this.   (Act V, Scene V)
14. Q. Brutus' wife is Portia, but there is also a more famous Portia in another of Shakespeare's plays. Which play?
    A. Portia of The *Merchant of Venice* saved Antonio from death at the hands of Shylock.
15. Q. Who struck the first blow when Caesar was killed?
    A. Casca.   (Act III, Scene I)
16. Q. Who complains, "Dwell I only in the suburbs of your pleasure?"
    A. Portia says to Brutus, "Dwell I but in the suburbs of your good pleasure?"   (Act II Scene I)
17. Q. Bernard Shaw wrote a play about Caesar; name it.
    A. *Caesar and Cleopatra*.
18. Q. What is the name of a very famous one-act play that is built around a line spoken by Julius Caesar?
    A. "Dear Brutus" is a three-act play written by J. M. Barrie. (Wrong.)
    A. *"The Valiant"* by Hall and Middlemass. (Correct.)
19. Q. What was Shakespeare's chief source for the play *Julius Caesar*?
    A. There is no indication that he used anything by way of source beyond Plutarch's *Lives* which he read in translation by Sir Thomas North.
20. Q. In twenty-five words or less, finish the sentence, I want to see the University Theatre's production of *Julius Caesar* because . . ."
    A. "I want to see the University Theatre's production of *Julius Caesar* because Shakespeare wrote magnificent passages of poised and skillful rhetoric for us to see and hear, not merely to read; this production offers us this opportunity."

An executive without adequate records may be compared to the man who is forever losing and hunting his keys. He never, never decides where to put them or how to find them. Consequently when he needs them in a hurry, everything is turned upside down to find what he should be able to put his fingers on in the dark.

Had it not been that someone cared enough about the future to keep a record, civilization would have made little progress. Great books such as the *Bible, Hamlet, Julius Caesar, Decline and Fall of the Roman Empire, Origin of Species, Canterbury Tales,* or even the recently discovered *Dead Sea Scrolls,* all these and hundreds more exist because someone kept a record. He may have been Herodotus, Homer, Plutarch, Bancroft, or someone completely unknown.

The intelligent use of good records will help us decide what to do as well as what not to do. If we fail to keep a record, how can we learn from experience? The successful operation of a theatre, like anything else, is more complicated and difficult than it looks, but a careful study of where we have been as well as where we are going may make the important difference of whether we sink or swim.

One parting word for the records: Let someone who really understands their function as well as their value be in *complete* charge of all of them. Records are to be used, and the more they are used the better; they are not to be put in the archives or the vaults. However, they should not be handed out for just anybody to work over. There must be a central responsibility for their preparation and care.

XVIII

THE ROUNDUP

When the big roundup is made on the cattle range, every animal is brought in. Sometimes it is a curious assortment of young and old, large and small, fat and thin, mavericks and well marked, regulars and freaks, mothers with their fat calves and the poor little orphaned dogies. They are all part of the herd. Often the wranglers are disturbed that certain prize animals are missing, for they know that either the roundup was not thorough enough or that cattle rustlers have stolen them. There must be some rechecking. The problem of what to do with the motley collection brings a lot of questions.

At the end of the theatre year, there should be a similar roundup and an inspection of the entire *omnium gatherum*. It is vital that such a roundup be undertaken in a thoroughly constructive atmosphere. It should not be merely a time to complain and to pass the buck. It should be a time to face problems honestly with open minds and good intentions. The first step in getting ready to assay and evaluate the program is to prepare a checklist of all items to be reviewed. Those which present little or no difficulty should be approved and checked off so as to move on to those which need attention. The following list is arranged as chronologically as possible; there is always overlapping, and sometimes it seems that everything should be done first:

Before the Show

1. Plan the budget.
2. Select the plays.
3. Get permission on play or get royalty quotations.
4. Set the dates.

5. Announce tryouts.
6. Price scale the house.
7. Order the tickets.
8. Plan advertising, including mailing list, newspaper, pictures, posters, and display boards.
9. Prepare the printed program—sell advertising space, check copy and proof.
10. Prepare box office.
    a. Select box office personnel.
    b. Rack tickets.
    c. Arrange operation schedule.
11. Check with house management on
    a. Ushers.
    b. Doormen.
    c. Ventilation.
    d. Parking lot supervision.
12. See that press, television, and radio courtesies are extended.
13. Prepare the pass list.
14. Contact newspaper reviewers.

During the Show

1. Revise newspaper advertisements.
2. Keep radio and television active with announcements and reviews.
3. Collect newspaper reports.
4. Meet the critics.
5. Check physical comfort of audience.
   a. Ventilation.
   b. Seating.
   c. Acoustics.
6. Keep house staff alerted.
7. Count tickets, check sales, make reports.
8. Study audience reactions.
9. Conduct any audience surveys.

After the Show

1. Make box office reports.
2. Send letters of appreciation.

3. Complete scrapbook and have it bound.
4. Pay the bills.
5. Gather up advertising boards, etc.; clean up.
6. Return all borrowed property.
7. Evaluate any suggestions.
8. Evaluate effectiveness of advertising.
9. Compile statistics on effectiveness of media used in selling tickets.
10. Discuss money-saving ideas.
11. Discuss changes in policy.
12. Review current financial status and consider reallocation.
13. Send exchange playbills to other theatres.
14. Note improvements made and improvements needed.
15. Present future plans.
16. Begin all over again.

With the list on the table for consideration, it is well to go all the way through it before starting the discussion. There will be a strong temptation to stop and discuss before the survey or roundup is really completed. While going through it a second time, assign the problems to the people who can best work with them. Before any changes are made, there should be a careful study. Sometimes changes are made just to be doing something. This can be dangerous. For example, someone who is not too well acquainted with the problem of pricing tickets says, "We need more revenue and I think that we ought to raise the price of the tickets to get it. The price of everything else has gone up; bread for instance has gone up four cents, milk three cents, and the utility bills have increased considerably. So I say, let's raise the price of the tickets." The speaker does not realize that his argument has a hole in it wide enough to drive a load of scenery through. Everyone may agree that more money is needed, but simply raising the price of the tickets has been known to produce the opposite result. People may have to buy bread and milk and pay the utility increase even if they don't want to, but they don't have to buy theatre tickets. Is there some other way? There must be.

A better approach would be to assign the question for a careful study by those closest to it. Recommendations would then be in order and would have substance to back them.

Since it would not be practicable to discuss the long list of topics, let us select three examples which may appear on most every theatre list: (1) first-night attendance, (2) passes, and (3) letters of appreciation.

1. *Poor attendance on the opening night* is one of the most universally troublesome problems. On this question the author made a roundup of expert opinions from directors and managers of more than fifty theatres. Some said that the problem could never be solved, but others said that they had already solved it. The following suggestions, for what they may be worth, represent some pretty thorough thinking by a great many experts:

a. Start with Friday and Saturday; omit Monday and Tuesday and play the other days.

b. Make the first night a gala occasion with lobby displays, introduction of important guests from the stage, dress up affair. This suggestion was made by several managers, one of whom said that the idea had taken hold with such success that first night invitations were sought after. Think of that!

c. Put all the passes on the first night and tighten up the list severely for any other night. Make a special effort to have a very favorable audience so as to impress the critics.

d. Have a big "meet the cast" party at the end of the show.

e. Plan a banquet early in the evening of the first night at which the dignitaries and theatre boosters are present. Send special invitations to leading people.

f. "We sell the fraternities and sororities first-night tickets on a 50-50 basis. This fills the house and they get money which they need."

g. Instruct all workers of the box office to put on an intensive campaign for the first night. Many undecided people can easily be persuaded. Ask the cast to push the first night rather than knock it. Players often say, "Oh, don't come the first night, our rehearsal was terrible."

h. Make it a privilege to attend by charging more.

i. Reduce the prices on the first and second night and raise them on the last nights.

j. Sell a large block of tickets to organizations at reduced rates, or let them keep part of the price of each ticket.

k. Don't advertise that you have a plethora of tickets, but develop the idea that they will be scarce and that they are going fast. Having plenty of tickets is a way of saying that there is a scarcity of patrons.

2. *The "pass list"* raises questions that recur annually. In a democratic institution questions should be out in the open. Everyone should have his say and let the policy be hammered out in the presence of those concerned. Then it should stand until the next roundup. A policy must be justified at least in the minds of those who make it. Otherwise, "There's no reason for it; it's just our policy," should be posted.

3. *Write letters of appreciation.* Failure to express appreciation is one of the most common oversights around the theatre. It is surprising what a lot of good will a timely, well-deserved note of appreciation will generate. In the theatre, as in any organization, many people give extremely important services with little or no monetary reward. What a difference it would make if a few of the officials took the time and made the effort to commend them. Sometimes these people are simply starved for a word of thanks, a word of praise. They don't ask to take a bow before the footlights or receive a round of applause, but they would like just a little recognition, and if they have done a good job, they should have it. Such notes take only a few moments, they cost almost nothing, and they help to keep the organization running smoothly. Some of the people who are often overlooked are radio announcers, janitors, stagehands, ushers, wardrobe workers, costumers, photographers, and newspapermen. A theatre director was once so impressed with the patience and courtesy of a newspaper photographer that he sent him a letter of sincere appreciation and a copy of it to the editor. The editor was delighted and commended the photographer who said, "Nothing like this ever happened to me before." The director who wrote the letter also felt better. Here was a bit of excellent public relations that did not cost a thing. Such simple expressions of gratitude do not seem to amount to much, but they may mean a great deal in an organization where we too often take our friends for granted. Cicero said, "Gratitude is not only the greatest of virtues, but the parent of all others."

The requisites for a successful director or manager are somewhat different from those of a successful actor or actress, but they are about as demanding. Ethel Barrymore listed six requirements for a successful actress: (1) The face of Venus, (2) the brains of Minerva, (3) the grace of Terpsichore, (4) the memory of Macaulay, (5) the figure of Juno, and (6) the hide of a rhinoceros.

The manager and director should have Numbers 4 and 6 plus the wisdom of Ulysses, and the speed of Mercury. Margo Jones said that for anyone who wishes to establish a theatre: "The word 'discouragement' must be eliminated from his vocabulary." That is a big order and few people can qualify.

Theatre people must be everlastingly resourceful. If one thing does not work, they turn to something else; but they don't stop. Show people are notorious for pulling themselves out of holes. The problem of keeping one's product before the public has long been recognized. In 45 B. C. Ovid said, "There is no desire for that which is unknown." When things get dull and one feels that he is being forgotten, a roundup of ideas for news stories may help:

Nominate a theatre queen.
Give an honor to someone.
Celebrate an anniversary.
Make a report.
Invite some group to visit your theatre.
Invite an eminent man in the field.
Announce a theatre trip.
Have an awards banquet.
Appear before the public.
Hold a reunion of former actors.
Entertain.
Stage a debate.
Commemorate some well-known week (International Drama Week).
Organize a community calendar.
Make a protest.
Write a letter of commendation.
Write a letter of complaint.
Announce a policy.
Report on a national theatre movement.
Give a benefit.

APPENDIX

Constitution

N B. (There is no standard constitution for any group or community. The following is only suggestive. A theatre should build its own constitution and by-laws to suit its own purposes.) In all such organizations there should be complete unity. The lines of communication between the manager and the director should be clear and open, but the two assignments should never interfere with each other. The constitution cannot be better than the spirit back of it.

ARTICLE I
The name of this organization shall be Fire Ball Theatre of Las Vegas.

ARTICLE II
The purpose of this group shall be to foster greater interest in the living theatre through the production of good plays. The study, reading, and staging of worthwhile dramatic works is to be encouraged.

ARTICLE III
Section 1. The officers shall consist of eleven members: President, Vice President, Secretary, Treasurer, and seven others.
Section 2. The directors shall be elected annually at the regular meeting of the members on the second Tuesday after the first day of May at 8 P.M. The officers shall be the controlling board of this theatre organization.
Section 3. In case of a vacancy occurring during the year, the officers shall appoint a member to fill the post, except the President, in which case the Vice-President automatically becomes the President.

ARTICLE IV
The membership of this theatre organization shall be unlimited.

ARTICLE V
The Constitution may be amended at any regular business meeting provided that the proposed amendment has been presented in writing at the previous business meeting.

By-Laws

ARTICLE I
Duties of the Officers

Section 1. The President shall preside at all meetings at which he is present, shall exercise general supervision over the affairs and activities of the organization and shall serve as a member ex-officio on all committees.

Section 2. The Vice-President shall assume all duties of the President in the latter's absence.

Section 3. The Secretary shall handle all correspondence, keep the minutes of meetings, and keep an accurate record of all business transacted.

Section 4. The Treasurer shall receive all monies and pay all bills from the funds of the organization as authorized by the board. The Treasurer shall keep an itemized account of receipts and expenditures.

ARTICLES II
Meetings

Section 1. Regular monthly meetings shall be held on the second Tuesday of each month in the theatre board room at 8 P.M.

Section 2. Any regular meeting may be postponed by the President with the concurrence of the Vice-President, Secretary, and Treasurer.

Section 3. Special meeting may be called at any time by the President and the Vice-President when the need arises.

   (Leaders of successful groups recommend a minimum of changes of dates allowed; regular meetings are important).

ARTICLE III

Two-thirds of the membership shall constitute a quorum to transact business, but less than two-thirds cannot transact official business.

ARTICLE IV

The following committees shall be appointed by the President:

(1) The Play Planning Committee will select all dates and plays. This committee will work in conjunction with the Director and Manager of the theatre.

(2) The New Membership Committee will work with the Promotion Department and coordinate the membership drive.

(3) Buildings and Grounds Committee will make recommendations concerning cleanliness, safety, and attractiveness of the building.

ARTICLE V
Equipment

No equipment shall be lent to any organization or individual without the expressed permission of the officers of the organization.

(Successful theatres have a stern policy on lending.)

ARTICLE VI

All funds shall be used for the producing of better plays, purchase of equipment, and for the general improvement of the theatre program.

THEATRE MANAGEMENT BIBLIOGRAPHY

Bernheim, Alfred L. *The Business of the Theatre*. New York: Actors Equity Association, 1932.

Dean, Alexander. *Little Theatre Organization and Management*. New York: Appleton and Company, 1926.

Ditton, William R. *A Survey of Publicity and Advertising Methods in College and University Theatre*. M.A. Thesis, Purdue University, 1957.

Green, Abel and Joe Laurie, Jr. *Show Biz*. New York: Doubleday & Co., 1953.

Guthrie, Tyrone. *A Life in the Theatre*. New York: McGraw-Hill, 1959.

Heffner, Hubert C., Selden, Samuel, and Sellman, Hunton D. *Modern Theatre Practice*. New York: F. S. Crofts & Co., 1939.

Hinsdell, Oliver. *Making The Little Theatre Pay*. New York: Samuel French, 1925.

Maytham, Thomas E. *Introduction to Advertising Principles and Practice*. New York: Harper & Brothers, 1948.

Neal, Robert M. *News Gathering and News Writing*. New York: Prentice-Hall, Inc. 1940.

Small Space Advertising. New York: Funk & Wagnalls Co. in association with Printers' Ink Publishing Co., 1948.

Smith, Milton. *Play Production*. New York: Appleton-Century-Crofts, 1948.

Sponseler, Whitney R. *A Manual for High School and College Theatrical Administration*. Hollywood: American Legitimate Theatre Service, 1956.

Stanton, Sanford E. *Theatre Management*. New York: Appleton-Century-Croft, 1939.

Whiting, Frank M. *An Introduction to The Theatre*. New York: Harper & Brothers, 1954.

Wright, Milton. *How to Get Publicity*. New York: McGraw-Hill, 1935.

Young, John Wray. *The Community Theatre*. New York: Harper & Brothers, 1957.

INDEX

Contributory negligence, 146
Copyrights for plays, 8, 107
Cosmetics, 173–193, *see* Make-up
Costume displays, 116
Crane, Dr. George W., study of book titles, 6
Critics' Reviews, 142
Curtains Going Up, 154

Date selection, advance selection, 27; calendars, 19, 28; competition consideration, 17–18; days of the week, 26; holidays, state and national, 20–25; weather, 26
Direct mail, 61–78
Directory of Newspapers and Periodicals, 155
Doorman, 134
Dramatics, 161
Dressing the house, 47

Educational Theatre Journal, 162
Encyclopedia of Exploitation, The, 156
Envelopes, for mailing, 68; prices of, 68; ticket envelopes, 42

Filing system for bookkeeping, 202
Film Daily Year Book, The, 157
First night attendance, 225

Glass Menagerie, comparative costs of production, 14
Glick, Carl, *Curtains Going Up*, 154
Gregory, Paul, 140, 157
Guide To Great Plays, A, 157

Handbills, *see* Posters
Hendricks, Bill, *Encyclopedia of Exploitation, The*, 156; *Showmanship in Advertising*, 158
Holidays, *see* Date selection

Impelling motives, 58–60
Incorporation for nonprofit theatres, 150
Insurance, A.N.T.A. information, 151; burglary and holdup, 151; compensation, 151; libel, 152; theatrical floater, 151
Invoice, 199

Laughton, Charles, 140, 157
Law, *American Jurisprudence*, 145; A.N.T.A., 151; bailment, 149; burglary and holdup insurance, 151–152; coat or checkroom, 148–150; compensation insurance, 151; contributory negli-

Law (*Continued*)
gence, 146; incorporation for nonprofit theatres, 150; insufficient illumination, 147; insurance, 150–151; invitee, 145; invitor, 145; lawsuits, 144; lawyers, 145; libel insurance, 152; licensee, 145; minor safety problems, 147; overcrowding the theatre, 146; public liability, 151; safe premises obligation, 145; theatre tickets, 147; theatrical floater, 151
Ledger, 202
Letters of appreciation, 226
Liability, *see* Law; *see also* Public liability
Lost and found department, 135

McCleery, Albert, *Curtains Going Up*, 154
Magill, Frank, *Masterplots*, 157
Mail, cost of, 67; envelopes, 68; first class, 65–66; fourth class, 66; second class, 66; third class, 66–67; what to mail, 68–71; when to mail it, 72
Mailing brochures, Catholic University sample, 73; copies for records, 214–215; San Jose State College sample, 75; University of California at Los Angeles sample, 76; University of Oregon sample, 77; University of Utah sample, 74; Wayne State University sample, 78
Mailing List, building a, 61–64; newcomers for, 63; post office check of a, 64–65; stenographic service used for, 63; telephone follow-up of, 102
Make-up, cold creams, 175–177; eye shadows, 189–190; grease paints, 177–183; hair blacking, 193; hair whiting, 192; lining materials, 187–188; liquid make-up, 183–185; powders, 190–192; rouges, 185–187; small scale manufacture of, 174; spirit gum, 193
Manager, 54–55, 134–135, 226
Margetts, Ralph, 165–173
Masterplots, 157
Match books, 116
Money saving devices, make-up, 173–193; props, 165–173

National Collegiate Players, *Players Magazine*, 163
National Thespian Society, The, *Dramatics*, 161
Newspapers, adjectives for advertising, 87; advertisement copies filed, 214;